Shelley Lasica
WHEN I AM NOT THERE

Published by
Monash University Museum of Art
Monash University Publishing

Monash University Museum of Art,
Monash University Publishing and Shelley Lasica
acknowledge the Boonwurrung, Wurundjeri
and Bunurong peoples of the Kulin Nation as
the first and continuing custodians of the lands
on which this project has been produced and
presented, and pay respect to Elders past, present
and emerging.

Foreword, Charlotte Day 5
WHEN I AM NOT THERE: An Introduction, Hannah Mathews and Lisa Catt 7
Prevailing Conditions, Shelley Lasica in Conversation with Claudia La Rocco 17
Shelley Lasica's Adventures with a Thing Called Choreography, Erin Brannigan 39
Shelley Lasica: Body of Work, Robyn McKenzie 63
Among and Against: Lasica's Contacts, Justin Clemens 83
Choreographing the Archive: Shelley Lasica's *WHEN I AM NOT THERE*, Zoe Theodore 101

Appearing to Create Something Solid 127
Turning Away the Affect of a Mystery 137
Now 153
BELIEVE 173
DRESS 181
The Idea of It 219

BEHAVIOUR Part 1 243
BEHAVIOUR Part 1 and 2 259
Here BEHAVIOUR Part 4 267
Square Dance BEHAVIOUR Part 6 277
BEHAVIOUR Part 7 293
CHARACTER X 306
live drama situation 340
SITUATION LIVE: THE SUBJECT 345
ACTION SITUATION 355
LIVE OPERA SITUATION 368
History Situation 375

VIANNE 396
VIANNE AGAIN 419
INSIDE VIANNE AGAIN (National Gallery of Victoria) 423

Solos for Other People 435
How Choreography Works 460
How How Choreography Works 467

The Shape of Things to Come 485
The Design Plot 515
Greater Union 599
If I Don't Understand You 615
WHEN I AM NOT THERE 635

Biography and Chronology 655
Bibliography 695
Creative Team 699
Contributors 701
Acknowledgements 701

Foreword, Barbara Kay

WHEN I AM NOT THERE: An Introduction, Hannah Mathews and Lisa Catt 3
Prevailing Conditions, Shelley Lasica in Conversation with Claudia La Rocco 11
Shelley Lasica: Who danced with a Thing Called Choreography, Erin Brannigan 19
Shelley Lasica: Bodies of Work, Robyn McKenzie 43
Actors and Agents in Lasica's Continuum, Tim Etchells 55
Choreographing the Archive, Shelly Lasica: WHEN I AM NOT THERE, For Elsewhere, for...

Appearing to Create Something Solid 127
Turning Away the Affect of a Mystery 137
Now 155
BELIEVE 173
DRESS 191
The Idea of It 215

BEHAVIOUR Part 1 243
BEHAVIOUR Part 3 and 2 259
Here BEHAVIOUR Part 4 267
Square Dance BEHAVIOUR Part 5 277
BEHAVIOUR Part 7 283

CHARACTER A 299
live drama situation 340
SITUATION LIVE: THE SUBJECT 345
ACTION SITUATION 355
LIVE OPERA SITUATION 365
History Situation 375

VIANNE 395
VIANNE AGAIN 419
INSIDE VIANNE AGAIN (National Gallery of Victoria) 423

Solos for Other People 455
How Choreography Works 469
How How Choreography Works 487

The Shape of Things to Come 495
The Design Plot 515
Greater Union 595
If I Don't Understand You 615
WHEN I AM NOT THERE 635

Biographical Chronology
Bibliography
Creative Team
Contributors
Acknowledgments

Foreword

While Shelley Lasica's *WHEN I AM NOT THERE* is part of a Monash University Museum of Art (MUMA) series that presents the work of influential Australian artists in depth, this project is also unique as the first curated survey of a choreographic practice in Australia. MUMA's Senior Curator Hannah Mathews has worked closely with Melbourne-based Lasica to devise a survey that is simultaneously a choreographic commission, where performers and objects (costumes, sculptures and sound compositions) share MUMA's gallery spaces for the duration of two weeks. The resulting performance–exhibition richly conveys the interdisciplinary, iterative nature of the choreographer and dancer's four-decade career, which has long engaged with art galleries and institutions and was recognised in 2021 with a prestigious Australia Council Fellowship.

As a museum located in a site of collaborative, interdisciplinary research and teaching, we are thrilled to be presenting the new ensemble work that Lasica has developed for this occasion with ten other artists: LJ Connolly-Hiatt, Luke Fryer, Timothy Harvey, Rebecca Jensen, Megan Payne, Lisa Radford, Oliver Savariego, Lana Šprajcer, François Tétaz and Colby Vexler. We are grateful for the dedication and engagement of this team of performers and consultants towards the realisation of this project, and recognise the creativity required to devise this new work during Melbourne's COVID-19 lockdown period. Special thanks go to Lasica's creative producer Zoe Theodore, who has provided steady support through this process.

This new commission has been co-commissioned by the Art Gallery of New South Wales with generous support from its benefactor group, Atelier. The performance–exhibition is part of a broader collaboration. It is MUMA's contribution to the three-year Australian Research Council Linkage Project *Precarious Movements: Choreography and the Museum*. The project affords MUMA and research partners Art Gallery of New South Wales, National Gallery of Victoria, Tate UK and University of New South Wales the opportunity for situated research on the curation and practice of choreography in the museum. We are delighted to collaborate on this critical project with our esteemed peers, and with Lasica as the project's Primary Research Associate.

I would like to thank Monash University Publishing for their partnership in this book project, the first monograph on a contemporary Australian choreographer. I extend thanks and congratulations to designers Stuart Geddes and Žiga Testen for capturing the movement and history of Lasica's practice through their design, and to Linda Michael and Clare Williamson for their meticulous editing and proofreading contributions. Sincere thanks to Hannah Mathews for her curatorial and editorial custodianship of the book and exhibition project, to Melissa Ratliff for her management of this publication, to MUMA/BAHC curatorial trainee Alice Mawhinney for her research support, and to all the writers for their insightful contributions.

We are grateful to Monash Art, Design and Architecture for providing rehearsal space during the development of this project. Among the many supporters, collaborators and lenders who have made this exhibition possible, I would like to finally thank the talented team at MUMA.

Charlotte Day
Director

WHEN I AM NOT THERE: An Introduction
Hannah Mathews and Lisa Catt

Since her first solo works made in the 1980s, Melbourne-based choreographer Shelley Lasica has experimented with the possibilities of dance, particularly by examining the various contexts in which it occurs. Her work has been presented in artist-run spaces, commercial galleries and museums as much as in conventional theatre spaces, nightclubs, rehearsal rooms and town halls. Crisscrossing space, for Shelley, is to crisscross the different value systems, expectations, modes and registers in which art happens. This enduring interest in the institutions and contexts of art extends from her close engagement with other disciplines and has been sustained by her many collaborators. Shelley's practice argues for art made at a nexus—and, for her, that nexus is dance.

The first dance artist to be represented by a commercial art gallery in Australia (at City Gallery, which became Anna Schwartz Gallery in 1992, from 1989 to 2006), Shelley has developed a body of work that is uniquely characterised by the conversations it holds with the traditions and practices of theatre, fashion, installation, painting, sound, sculpture, literature, architecture and dance itself, to present a non-exclusive list. These conversations serve to create both a physical and relational infrastructure within her practice. As explored by Robyn McKenzie, a writer and past collaborator of Shelley's, who is one of the contributors to this book, this infrastructure has been fundamental to her work from the very outset—from her upbringing with her choreographer mother to her undergraduate studies in art history and her emergence within the experimental, artistic milieu of 1980s Melbourne.

Given Shelley's long-standing engagement with choreography, dance and the sites and behaviours of the art gallery, it was inevitable that her practice became a focus of the recently announced Australian Research Council Linkage Project, *Precarious Movements: Choreography and the Museum*. Monash University Museum of Art (MUMA) and the Art Gallery of New South Wales are contributors to this project, alongside the National Gallery of Victoria, Tate UK and the University of New South Wales, with Shelley as Primary Research Associate. Shelley has been critical to the project, as both advocate and artist. Her contribution has ensured that the concerns of practice are embedded within each stage of the research—from the principles through to the process. Her involvement has fostered understanding of the unique concerns and methodologies that have propelled her own practice, but also foregrounded the work of other dance artists and choreographers, both in Australia and overseas, who have recently begun working with the art museum.

Moreover, now entering her fifth decade of making work at the intersection between dance and the visual arts, Shelley holds a most valuable perspective on what it means to be carrying out this research at this time. She is able to place the thread of our investigation within a lived lineage of attitudes, histories, trends and practices. If there is anyone who can offer an answer to the question 'What is dance today?'—as posed by Justin Clemens in his chapter 'Among and Against'—it is Shelley.

With the additional support provided by Australian Research Council funding, in early 2021 MUMA invited Shelley to present a survey exhibition that would comprise an exhibition, a new commission and a publication. This occasion marked a number of firsts: the first survey of an Australian choreographer by a museum and the first monograph of a contemporary Australian choreographer—both pointing to an oversight that has rendered contemporary dance particularly precarious in this country. Importantly for Shelley, it also provided an opportunity to undertake a major new commission that could continue her research and investigation into dance and its meanings while simultaneously reflecting on the relationships between choreography and the museum; the archive and an oeuvre.

The significance of this invitation was not lost on Shelley who quickly set about developing the new commission during the COVID-19 pandemic of 2020–22. The work soon found its title *WHEN I AM NOT THERE*—a statement that strikes at a tension at the very heart of the invitation: How to escape the tyranny of the museum survey reducing performance practice to only its documentation? Working in close conversation with dancers LJ Connolly-Hiatt, Luke Fryer, Timothy Harvey, Rebecca Jensen, Megan Payne, Lana Šprajcer and Oliver Savariego; creative producer Zoe Theodore; sound artist François Tétaz; and consultants Lisa Radford and Colby Vexler, Shelley fashioned a language for the new work that declared its contingent nature: performance–exhibition. The new commission would attend to the spatial, temporal and communication conventions of the museum, while also distilling Shelley's archive of movement, research and methodology via a range of pedagogical approaches and generative structures with the dancers and consultants.

It is worth noting here the importance of relationships to the way Shelley makes art. She is always thinking about how to work with people. How do you establish collaborations that allow for both exchange and agency? What does it mean to situate and negotiate oneself with and against another? One must first understand where knowledge lies in the body, and then work out how to transmit that knowledge. Shelley has deftly articulated these ideas across her practice as she has moved between working as a solo performer and making large-scale ensemble works. The possibilities of translation, and for mistranslation, have become generative for her practice.

For the new commission, Shelley wanted to draw upon existing relationships but also forge new ones. Her methods of establishing and re-establishing these relationships for the new work are detailed in the chapter 'Choreographing the Archive' by Zoe Theodore. Here Zoe provides insight into the artist's thinking throughout the commissioning process. We are invited into the internal mechanism of the work as Shelley figures out what the work needs to be or to become.

The proposition of a performance–exhibition piqued the interest of the Art Gallery of New South Wales, which saw it as a welcomed provocation. Moreover, in a sentiment shared with MUMA, it recognised the importance of pairing its research commitment with an active demonstration of supporting dance practice—that it must learn and do. Thanks to the generosity of its benefactor group, Atelier, the Art Gallery was able to join MUMA as co-

commissioner for the new work. Establishing this partnership between Shelley, MUMA and the Art Gallery felt right for the commission, as it ensured that the invitation would uphold a central tenet of Shelley's practice—to take on different contexts and test the conditions of different spaces.

WHEN I AM NOT THERE is to be presented within the galleries during usual opening hours, growing from a single dancer to an ensemble of eight in the space. At MUMA it will take up all gallery spaces, while at the Art Gallery it will be presented alongside other exhibitions in the contemporary galleries. In both cases, at times, there will be multiple activities in various rooms happening simultaneously, with the performance taking place with a mise-en-scène incorporating objects, including moveable screens, an armature for costumes and a sound score.

Audience members will be invited to situate themselves within, or at a distance from, the performance—to be as proximate as they please. Dance writer and academic Erin Brannigan addresses the processes of spectatorship in her chapter 'Shelley Lasica's Adventures with a Thing Called Choreography', identifying the co-presence of performers and audiences within Shelley's work. Shelley is deeply interested in how the audience sees things, creating multiple points of view so that we are engaging with what is not visible as much as with what we can see. This aspect of her practice is mused upon in *WHEN I AM NOT THERE*—costumes and objects offer places for performers to hide within the work.

The survey element of the invitation made to Shelley by MUMA posed a curatorial challenge and in the context of the ARC *Precarious Movements* project a valued opportunity for experimentation. By their nature, surveys are often a much desired yet confronting process: a deep reflection back across an artist's practice that looks closely at ideas, method, sites, relationships and research, seeking to distil a narrative or process that can be communicated to a broad audience—one that reveals the complexity and challenges of a long-term practice rather than a heroic trajectory from A to B. To survey a practice that is primarily somatic and embodied, despite its commitment to a strong visuality, required a truly collaborative approach. Shelley and Zoe Theodore shared their time, resources and ideas generously, making accessible Shelley's extensive archive and providing introductions to a network of collaborators.

As the first survey of an Australian choreographer, and in complementing the major commission being developed in parallel, it was essential that the curatorial contribution to *WHEN I AM NOT THERE* met the longevity and significance of Shelley's practice. It was important that it didn't default to the curatorial methodologies used in previous choreographic surveys, such as those of Michael Clark at the Barbican (2020) or Merce Cunningham at the Walker Art Center (2017), where various parts of the practice (costumes, sets, documentation and the re-performance of works) were broken apart, categorised and separated across spaces to become fixed and historicised documents of the work.

The resulting curatorial approach at MUMA drew on Shelley's original concept for a performance-exhibition and a desire to locate the live performance with a mise-en-scène: a total approach where one element could

not exist without the other, and where contingency was acknowledged and not dismissed. In consultation with Shelley, a curated selection of items, images, texts and sounds were distilled from her archive to populate the galleries, with each element carefully selected to reference various and recurring presences within Shelley's practice, its works, locations and collaborators.

These include: original artworks by others that featured in her earlier works, such as Callum Morton's *Twister* video, 1999, Kathy Temin's wearable soft sculpture for *CHARACTER X*, 1996, Tony Clark's paintings for *BELIEVE*, 1990–91, and sculptures by Anne-Marie May; original costumes by designers such as Kara Baker, Martin Grant, Richard Nylon and Belinda Hellier previously worn by Shelley and her dancers; items that index or reference materials that have appeared in earlier works, such as the blue Tarkett flooring similar to that used in *Here BEHAVIOUR Part 4*, 1995, or the translucent green film applied to the museum's window that filters the natural light to a hue that recalls Roger Woods's fluorescent tubes in *Square Dance BEHAVIOUR Part 6*, 1996–97; writing that has preceded or responded to Shelley's works, such as Robyn McKenzie's script for *SITUATION LIVE: THE SUBJECT*, 1997–98, and Jacqui Shelton's text for *The Design Plot*, 2017–, transferred to video; and a soundscape by François Tétaz that includes existing scores by Tétaz and Milo Kossowski.

With the exception of the costumes that will be worn at various times during the daily performances, these materials may or may not be used by the dancers. Instead, they function simultaneously as an expanded mise-en-scène for a performance and an exhibition of items that survey a practice: collapsing any reading of them as existing or new, historical or contemporary, artwork or prop.

Aligned with the ambiguity of the performance-exhibition we are looking at, there are none of the usual labels on the gallery walls. In their place a room sheet provides information on the provenance of each item in the space and its significance in Shelley's oeuvre, along with full acknowledgement of the contribution of others in her work. Thus language, here too, appears and disappears from the space. Shelley is interested in written language and its structures as much as she is in choreographic language. This is something that is thoughtfully explored in the chapter 'Prevailing Conditions', a conversation between Shelley and writer Claudia La Rocco that meanders from the qualities of tone and texture in both their practices to the meaning of 'meaning' in both dance and writing. Indeed, Shelley's adoption of the room sheet allows for a deferred mediation and a focus on meaning rather than understanding.

Shelley refers to families, relatives and clusters when discussing her works and the materials that shape them. These connections—relations—are demonstrated both in the writing commissioned for this publication and in its illustrated plates section. Here Shelley's four, nearly five, decades of practice and her distinct visual style are captured in a range of images that are gathered in five sections that collectively trace Shelley's body of work.

The first covers her early period, characterised by an interest in understanding the solo form as distinct from working with others, its specific address of the audience and how it might be distributed outside the usual dance network. We then move through images of the formative *BEHAVIOUR* and *Situation* series extending across two decades and marking her central concern

with spaces and their particular typologies, along with her decisive move from solo to ensemble works and the appropriation of narrative devices. The third section is dedicated to the *VIANNE* series where, within an austere funding climate, Shelley re-imagined how to redo a single work in different ways and in different places.

The fourth section takes us to two key works of 2015, *How Choreography Works* and *Solos for Other People*, which demonstrate Shelley's persistent questioning and unwavering curiosity about how to work with dancers. The final section covers her most recent cluster—*The Design Plot*, *Greater Union*, 2018–20, and *WHEN I AM NOT THERE*, works interconnected in their focus on establishing complex embodied systems that can be repeated in different contexts. This section also acknowledges Shelley's surprise return to solo work, with the archly titled *The Idea of It*, 2006, and a re-performance of *DRESS*, 1998, more conventionally choreographic in their arrangement.

This visually charged section of the publication elaborates Shelley's enduring interest in the context and situations of presenting choreography and in its collaborative and interdisciplinary possibilities. Through the lens of each photographer she has worked with, images trace and reveal the evolution of her ideas, conversations, collaborations and investigations with space and audience. Here, the ambiguity that characterises and is held tightly in much of Shelley's work is captured and stilled by images.

Shelley acknowledges that context is everything and that between one work and the next she is following ideas, negotiating current concerns, and sometimes even remaking the same work within a different set of conditions. Her practice is not populated or propelled by the new, but by relationships, systems, writing and research, by working through how things connect and how she works. As this publication and accompanying exhibition and commission attest, Shelley is remarkably adept and committed to making things happen.

Prevailing Conditions Shelley Lasica in Conversation with Claudia La Rocco

I met Shelley five years ago, when I first travelled to Australia to teach a writing workshop as part of the 2017 Dancehouse Dance Massive public program; I returned in 2020 for more teaching, just before the pandemic shut things down, and had the pleasure to work with her again. We've not spent many hours together, all things considered, but those hours have been rich, full of somatic and spoken conversations in and around and under the relationship between dance and writing—or maybe it's better to think of it as one long conversation, with various iterations. This latest one took place during January and February of 2022, Melbourne to Oakland.

CLAUDIA LA ROCCO

I've just done your warm-up on page 167 of *To Note: Notation Across Disciplines*, a book given to me by one of the participants in the first workshop I taught in Melbourne.[1]

Actually I haven't done your warm-up yet. I was about to, and then I realised I wanted to record myself saying it so I didn't have to be reading while doing the exercise, and then I realised this was what we should or would or could be talking about: How things translate and don't translate, how different technologies allow things to travel, what gets lost, what remains.

I think many people would agree that the book is a pretty good technology, and I would argue that dance as well is an excellent technology. So resilient, the strength of that resiliency built into change and distortion. The foundational idea of mutability—from body to body, performance to performance, experience to memory—is so different from conventional notions of visual art preservation or even of so much publishing; far from being a shortcoming, I find it to be a great attribute, and absolutely liberatory.

So now, here I go, to enact (perform?) a version of a Wednesday 9 December 2015 warm-up by Shelley Lasica, her voice to my eyes to my mouth to my ears. Starting.

1—Hannah Mathews (ed.), *To Note: Notation Across Disciplines*, Perimeter Editions, Melbourne, 2017.

SHELLEY LASICA

Ha, I can't remember the details of that warm-up. I will have to find the book and look at it. By the way, I most certainly did do your first workshop—it was great, and I have to say considerably different, or at least

it had a different focus, from the other two. Much more on writing about particular work, but still with a very strong focus on the act of writing and its relationship with a physical sensing and enquiry.

This translation issue especially between media is really generative for me at the moment in working on my current project, *WHEN I AM NOT THERE*—not only the idea of working between and with other modes of communication and practice but also thinking about their particular relationships and possibilities. After working with the seven other performers this last week after the summer break, I have been talking with the two consultants working with me, Lisa Radford (artist and writer) and Colby Vexler (architect undertaking a master's degree in the School of Culture and Communication, University of Melbourne), about objects and this thing I keep on inanely calling 'the crisis of objects'. This crisis is one of the initial themes I was thinking about, especially in relation to the title I began with when thinking about this work several years ago: *GO FIGURE: TO FIGURE*. I am really interested in the various dictionary meanings of the word 'figure', both as a verb and as a noun, and their relationship to what I am doing at Monash University Museum of Art with *WHEN I AM NOT THERE*, which exists sort of simultaneously as a performance and as an exhibition.

CLR

Here is a picture of the warm-up. I sent the voice memo I recorded to a friend of mine who has just sustained a bad injury and cannot walk. I thought he might like to do some of it in his imagination: that Feldenkrais idea I love so much, that to imagine is better than to do, some (most?) times.[2]

Here is also a photo of notes I took just now, while watching a video of your *Solos for Other People*, 2015. I decided after I started that I would send it to you and that I wanted it to fit on one page—two decisions that changed the notes, probably for the worse. You can see where my handwriting became aware it had an audience, at any rate. I am not sure what made me write 'the imagination as mistranslation', or even what it means, entirely (memory as mistranslation certainly—maybe there isn't much difference). But I wonder if it resonates for you at all, negatively or positively or otherwise?

I looked up 'figure' on the internet; my favourite phrase in the definition is 'representing something other'.

2—Feldenkrais is an educational system that uses movement to teach self-awareness and improve bodily function.

Would you say more about the crisis of objects? (Your use of 'inanely' made me laugh.) And/or what is happening for you in the studio today, as you imagine *WHEN I AM NOT THERE*'s future as performance and exhibition?

SL

I guess I am thinking crisis because this is something I have a feeling of anxiety about—but it is really a riddle or a conundrum, something unsolvable, although much spoken of and written about in various realms.

Imagination as mistranslation ... well, maybe there are various modes of remembering at play almost simultaneously, or they tumble and evoke each other in varying orders. Some are almost like smells, evoking a very particular mood or moment in time; some are kinaesthetic and feel deeply embedded in physical experience; and some are analytical, organised and structured. I don't really know if any of them are any more reliable than the others, but they seem to work together.

You used the word 'texture' in your notes about *Solos for Other People*. This is a word that comes up for me again and again, as does 'tone'—they are really helpful in thinking about building a work and performing, two aspects of the same thing. These words are complicated and, like other words often associated with other media, they are loaded and full of potential when discussed in a choreographic context. I guess I don't use them in an expressive way but maybe in a way that relates to materiality.

In the same way, the word 'figure' offers me the possibility to think about its many meanings in relation to different modes of communicating—as an action or a description, and most importantly, as equipment to exercise this idea of 'meaning'. And I guess we get back to translation again. Not everything translates.

But back to 'figure' and its definitions—variously, but not only: number, a person's body, power, modes of thinking, money, perspective, shape, diagram, pattern, motif—and its resonance within art language, especially 'figure and ground' in painting. Thinking about exhibition and performance in one breath but also understanding that you might choke ... Performance and exhibition are not a smooth (swallowable) mix in my mind, but together describe a thing in itself that bristles with the logic of each form. They are not interchangeable, but they can inflect and annoy each other.

Let me think more about objects ...

CLR

Texture and tone, yes! Those are such important words for me as well—paramount in good writing, or the writing that moves me, at least. I think that's why dance resonated for me so strongly (contemporary, non-narrative dance—argh, adjectives, I don't even like those ones, but maybe just to put us in a neighbourhood), because it was so clear to see the kinship between poetry and dance, that they both are driven by these engines of texture, tone, space, rhythm. My formal education was in literature, much of it poetry, and I often say that I learned to write by watching dance; it was a great gift to begin working as a dance critic in my early twenties, seeking to translate into words the often wordless poetics of fully developed artists while I was just beginning to sort myself out as a writer.

I think most things don't translate. And when we get interested in the possibilities of those gaps and failures and mistakes, that's when we can really start cooking with language—whether written, movement, sound, visual ...

I like thinking of how the exhibition and performance can annoy each other. That's great. In the United States there is the chronic discussion of dance 'activating' or 'complicating' the white box (which doesn't say much about what the white box is prior to such an intervention); perhaps at one point that language was alive, but at this point it feels pretty dead. It's—well, it's annoying, for starters! I appreciate the minor key, the way neighbours might annoy each other over time.

I just watched you 'Being John' for a while ... I love the sense of nonchalance, how decisions seem to be made or unmade at moments.[3] It's a pleasure to watch you move. Languid vectors in space. Just before that I had looked at flyers, and now am imagining what the spaces were in *BEHAVIOUR*, and how people in turn acted. And then I opened this review: yes! Perfect advice.[4]

I am thinking that I perhaps don't think much about objects, in art, that is. Though I do love the idea (and [un]reality) of found objects—more so in writing or dance (and/or live art generally), less so when it comes to actual objects.

3—'Being John' is one of the 'fragments' from, or source material for, Lasica's work *VIANNE* (first performed in 2008) that is also present in *WHEN I AM NOT THERE*.

4—Editor's note: This refers to a fragment of the article by Stephanie Glickman, 'Throw Caution to the Wind', *Herald Sun*, 16 February 1999. The excerpt features the word 'Throw' (from the headline) in large type and the first line of the review: 'To enjoy *Action Situation*, one must abandon the need to grasp narrative and submit to ambiguity.'

SL

I love how you have made a detail of this advice from a reviewer! The word that strikes me most though is 'Throw'... one of those words that you look at on the page and it starts to lose sense; say it many times with many different nouns attached to it and it becomes a dynamic system of activity that creates new possibilities for understanding.

Yesterday I was talking with Lisa and Colby and although the conversations were separate my ideas accumulated across the two meetings and they seem apt to our conversation.

Lisa and I had been talking about some practical and logistical issues to do with the performance and how it will unfold over the hours and days of the exhibition, and the relationship between some of the items from earlier work that will be present in the space and serve as kind of convertibles, functioning as costumes and objects and referring directly to themselves at that moment, while historically connecting to earlier works in which they were once situated. We went over the organisation of timetables, rosters of people performing and also the structure of the work in chapters, the layout of the different spaces in the gallery and their particularities, the opening hours, etc. These practical considerations are enormously interesting in the making of the work and are what I would call something like 'prevailing conditions'. They speak to the logic of the work, the nature of institutional activities, and the real lives of the people involved, while never being about them.

Colby was talking about the idea of 'understanding' rather than 'meaning', with respect to architecture and then choreography, which I thought was a really useful distinction as we approach ways of interacting with those coming to attend the work. It also is interesting in relation to the little text you plucked. Rather than a restriction in the possibilities of meaning, I think choreography in and of itself has the potential to engage with meaning in a very complex way, one that allows for so many modes of apprehension, but somehow resists completion—maybe. Or maybe I am speaking more specifically about the work I am interested in making.

'Being John' is a personal reference to the film *Being John Malkovich* and the way in which the actor plays 'himself'. It deals with the choreographic conundrum of material—variously taught, passed or given to, interpreted for or shared with other performers—both in relation to the building of works and the idea of legacy. I am not 'Being John' so much as being myself, with the purpose of asking the dancers to 'be me' in the mode of the film (impersonating, copying, embodying me)—not something I would generally ask of the performers, but this is about going there and finding out what choreographic knowledge is and isn't.

It is a provocation; at different times and in slightly different ways over the last nearly fifteen years I have asked people to learn this material with the idea of 'being me'. The section is improvised, and done specially for the camera, a tool for a certain type of learning. I wanted to use this film of me as material for dancers to approach indexically or as a self-revealing mechanism. What I was interested in was a relationship to learning material. I work a lot with improvising in different modes and containers: I am always fascinated with watching everyone else and myself learn themselves and learn me—it is a very particular relationship to kinaesthetic and analytical thinking. Somehow this thing or device (the video that is shot by me of myself undertaking a five-minute sequence of dance) functions as a kind of key for me in a number of works. Also, over the passage of time, the video itself has become important in its own terms. It exemplifies the tension between improvisation and choreography in the making of the 'Being John' phrase. While carefully considered and structured, it was nonetheless improvised specifically for the camera. So that somehow the hierarchy of 'performance' and 'document' is confounded. As a piece of movement to learn it is infinitely generative. This confounded object is also a resistance to unison and the presumptions that this mode often insists on—conformity, an indistinguishable identity to 'dancer' that reduces an individual's agency as a performer. Contrarily, it invites the viewer to compare performers on a very restricted scale of merit. Of course there are choreographers who work with unison in entirely different ways.

I guess this reveals one of the ongoing discussions I have with myself in making work, about the relationship between choreography which is made and performed solo and that which involves a number of people. And then we return again to translation!

And to the world of objects ... Objects are so complex: the presumption of use and utility, the tension between their intrinsic nature and their function in relation to humanness. Let alone their gift for symbolism and the endless, mutable ways we individually and collectively apprehend them.

CLR

Yes! And especially the prominence of that one word, THROW, which, out of context, makes it more into an object than a word would perhaps normally be. Your

phrase 'dynamic system of activity' makes me think of how words often function as placeholders for steps/sequences/sections in a choreographic process, inscrutable (to outsiders)—phrases that, for those making the dance, signal and help to locate entire and intensely specific movement terrains.

You write: 'Rather than a restriction in the possibilities of meaning, I think choreography in and of itself has the potential to engage with meaning in a very complex way, one that allows for so many modes of apprehension, but somehow resists completion—maybe. Or maybe I am speaking more specifically about the work I am interested in making.' YES. Big yes for this. Again, linking right back to the sort of writing that I am interested in: most obviously poetry, though not necessarily and not always. There is that old saying: 'in prose, we stop reading when we don't understand; in poetry, when we do', and so one never stops, really, because there is always more to understand. I think the word 'porous' has become something of a cliche in talking about dance, but it's really apt: so many ways to enter and exist [ha, I meant to type 'exit', but this also is true]. Room to breathe. And I think the things we are saying about dance and text could easily be swapped; they share so much. Perhaps not more than other art forms, perhaps (probably?) it's just these are the two I know best.

To loop back to the thought of 'throw' as an object, and to your last paragraph above, I'm now thinking of how often dance artists say to me in workshops that they find written language difficult, even oppressive, because it's so definitive and solid—whereas my sense of what words can (and cannot) do on a page, when words are really cooking creatively that is, is so much closer to what you write about objects' gift for symbolism and how endless and endlessly mutable our interpretations are; in this alone there is never the possibility of a word being definitive nor solid. There are only the gaps in understanding, rich with possibility and pleasure.

I wish I could see one of the exhibition spaces you are describing. For now, I am populating it with aspects of your previous works that I have seen, and your words here that my imagination is translating. There's now something fuzzy going on with John M. and that gold material on the floor in *Solos for Other People*.

This seems like a good time to watch *If I Don't Understand You*, 2019, a work you made a few years ago. So that's what I'm doing now. There's so much concentric

movement: dancers within camera-people within audience members within cameras within viewer ... so much (many) science fiction(s).

SL

I will respond later in the day but off to rehearsal now ...

The naming of things in the studio—particular modes of thinking in developing movement material (flavours) and also particular parts of the work—is a kind of index system for us and one that happens in every studio, I think. For *WHEN I AM NOT THERE* these named parts will become the chapters that make up the work.

In using the word 'chapters', I am coopting a word from literature (via the artist R.H. Quaytman) as a way of thinking about repetition, memory, and developing a type of order—a different kind of pattern recognition. Quaytman uses the word 'chapters' to title exhibitions. In the works she makes she directly invokes the history of painting, literature and thinking as a system, and somehow the way they differ and connect is poignant for me.

Languages and understanding ... What do I mean when I say 'understand'? I have made several works based on situations in which people either thought they were understanding each other or completely misread situations or interpreted them differently or had different valences and contexts—kind of watershed moments or, in fact, just day-to-day communications between people reliant on the wild assumption that we understand each other. Hence my work *If I Don't Understand You*. I am so interested in misunderstandings at the moment, or when people misconstrue—particularly in texting communications, when you lack context—an extreme version of this!

Not sure what the 'fuzzy thing going on with John M. and that gold material on the floor' is ... but I will return to your mistyping of 'exit' as 'exist' and think about how both words function in choreography as framing devices—not only in the ways of building and making the material, the movement of performers together, but also in the way that this information can be gathered and reflected on by the person attending. Because whichever way you cut it, choreography, and dance particularly, exists in time in all its possibilities. What structures and references may be sufficiently potent to allow the experience of

attending a performance to become an idea, a line of thought, an area of attention?

We had a conversation in the studio the other day about the legacy of particular cultural milieus as well as the legacy of an individual's practice. Sometimes the passing on of choreographic information relates to hierarchical modes that are seemingly in conflict with the spirit of the endeavour: I suppose the conversation was about power and control, a very messy and interesting area. It then became also about the structure of our working relationship and being able to work at a particular part of *WHEN I AM NOT THERE* in a different way.

CLR

I had to go back to my previous entry to remember the 'fuzzy thing' and even then was like, 'CLR, what??' Slowly (re?)constructing my meaning, this phrase was my placeholder for expressing what was happening in my imagination when I 'looked' at your exhibition ...

Gathered and reflected, yes! And refracted ... This reminds me of the debate within criticism over a writer speaking from the artist's intentions versus the audience member's understanding or misunderstanding of those intentions. Probably obvious to you: I've always been more engaged with the latter perspective, whether I'm the critic or the artist. The idea of reading the press release as guide/guardrails for my imagination in the encounter with someone else's work seems like some form of soft, self-imposed authoritarianism that doesn't end well for anyone. (Similar to the objective/subjective debate ...)

I've long felt that all art forms essentially exist through time and space; at least those made by mortal creatures like us: dance only throws this inevitability into deliciously sharp relief—as you say, 'time in all its possibilities'.

God, yes, re hierarchical modes of working being at odds with stated ideals of work. It's one of the great, dark hypocrisies of the art world. Do as we say ...

SL

Regarding the artist's intention and audience response, whose responsibility it is to know ... well, I am interested in context and also in the ongoing discussions around how much, what sort of, and in what form information is necessary for a person to enter a work. I suppose I am

very interested in the idea of framing, particularly in embedding that in the work, while understanding that all I can (or want to) do is provide—through various mechanisms—an open invitation to engage actively. This may have little to do with my intentions in the work; this triangulation between me, the work and the person engaging with it (in an active way that might bring surprises for them and for me if I am party to their response) is endlessly fascinating and has little to do with 'insider knowledge'.

I've been thinking about how time functions in relation to objects as a kind of way of thinking about choreographic potential rather than solution. I guess one of my big interests in imagining through other media (writing, cinema, visual art forms, exhibitions) is to pull things around as much as possible by working with their similarities and differences and their respective logics.

I never really know if I am working in the same way or differently from how I worked another time—probably a bit of both—but what keeps me going on is often something that irritates me, something that makes me try to work out how to make choreography function in a particular set of circumstances, with restrictions and potentialities. A huge part of this is the performers that I engage with to develop the work.

We have just completed a cycle of studio time in the lead-up to the presentation of *WHEN I AM NOT THERE*, and over the last year I have been working with a variety of choreographic and dancing practices that are simultaneously a kind of training and a container for us all to work together and establish, more than anything, a mode of working. All the performers bring with them their technê, their experiences and interests, as they establish their relationship to the work and their agency within it.

The relationships we have between ourselves and with the work are complex and shifting. We work in bursts—I like to space out working periods for this scale of production to allow things to filter around and shift and layer. During the pandemic this happened as we walked and talked, or read, discussed and posted online. But most of all in this process is how the relationship is a strange mixture of pedagogical, communal and tangential learning, distribution of information and gathering of a kind of web of knowledge together. I ceased being interested in teaching people to 'move like me' either in form or texture as the sole way of building performances a

long time ago. But *something* passes between us and in building *WHEN I AM NOT THERE*—because of the long research time and the possibilities for exhibition/performance offered through MUMA's commission—it feels like this mechanism is especially juicy.

CLR

I appreciate that you posit the relationship between you, your work and the person engaging with the work as a triangulation; I used to think of criticism as a triangulation between me, another person's work and the world. I suppose there's no real reason to stop at that geometric shape (one could add time, for example). But triangles for me evoke a certain generative motion, energy travelling through those three circuits.

There is so much more to say!—not in this conversation, alas, as we are up against our word limit and time constraints (speaking of a particular set of circumstances).

Thank you so much for this exchange.
A most pleasurable collaboration across and through time and space.

long time ago. But a sublime press-between us was fine-
building WITH A TWO-SOFTHERE-because of the long
research time and the possibilities for emulation /
performance sketch through MIDMAS commissions. It
feels like this mechanism is especially fitted.

cts

I appreciate that you posit the relationship between
your work and the notion engaging with the work
as a triangulation. Based to think of software as a
triangulation between me, another person/artist, and
the world, I suppose that's no real reason to stop at that
geometric shape (one God!) and three, four, simple.
But triangles for me evoke a certain generative motion,
energy, travelling through those three circuits.
There is so much more to say—not in this
conversation, Reis, as we are up against our very limit
and time constraints (speaking the particular set of
circumstances).
 Thank you so much for this exchange.
A most pleasurable collaboration across and through
time and space.

Shelley Lasica's Adventures with a Thing Called Choreography
Erin Brannigan

The thing, it is the now the thing the thingness of choreography now it is the thing that is not a thing. That's the whole point.
—Shelley Lasica[1]

It's early morning in the Art Gallery of New South Wales, Sydney, and Shelley Lasica and I are almost the only people in the entrance court. Lasica is scoping the space in preparation for a performance the next day and some photos I snapped at the time call back my memory of this moment. They have also become a visual cue for some other thoughts about Lasica that I expand upon here. At the time, my uncanny experience of an empty museum mashed with Lasica's physical behaviour as the lone soul in my sights. She didn't do much. She was standing, walking, moving gently in other ways—a twist of her hips, an extended arm—but I could see that her attention was dispersed. She was taking in the whole environment: the hard marble floor, the vast space lit from the harbour end of the building with sharp light bouncing off water and through glass, the other art on the expansive walls around her, the hum of the escalator at the far end. Looking at the images I am struck by the slightness of her frame within the space. Lasica and the institution meeting in a quiet moment but not without trouble.

Rehearsal images, Shelley Lasica (pictured), Deanne Butterworth and Jo Lloyd, *How How Choreography Works* 2016, Art Gallery of New South Wales, Sydney, 26 April 2016. Background: Paintings by Ildiko Kovacs. Photos: Erin Brannigan

* * *

Since her first work in a gallery, *Describing the perspective of time, It promises you nothing*, at Reconnaissance Gallery, Melbourne, in 1986, Lasica has presented shows in a theatre a handful of times in comparison to innumerable works in different types of spaces, including galleries. She is an artist who, from one

1—Shelley Lasica, 'Do You Do This Often?', *Performance Paradigm*, vol. 13, 2017, p. 211, https://www.performanceparadigm.net/index.php/journal/article/view/202/199.

vantage point, can be understood in relation to a unique lineage of women who recalibrated their discipline: dance artists committed to corporeal practices which they adapted in dialogue with progressive elements in the contemporary arts. Lasica started her public dance career as she meant to go on, beyond the confines of dance in its traditional disciplinary profile and pre-empting major aesthetic shifts at the interface between dance and visual art.[2] Lasica's oeuvre (1978–2022, to date) embraces the real risk of invention that tests medium-based 'grammatical' conventions, the kind of risk-taking that has been foundational to the post-disciplinary condition of contemporary art in the twenty-first century. To understand Lasica's position within local and international art contexts we can look back a few decades at some precedents, but I will also turn to some very tenacious yet soft-focus memories of my first encounters with Lasica's work at Performance Space in Sydney in the late 1990s, as programmed by Angharad Wynne-Jones. I'm also interested in how Lasica's choreography 'works' (to quote the title of *How Choreography Works*, 2015, created by Lasica with Deanne Butterworth and Jo Lloyd), and the early solo pieces I encountered at that time provide a clear view of some concerns that persist, circling around the elements of behaviour and form.

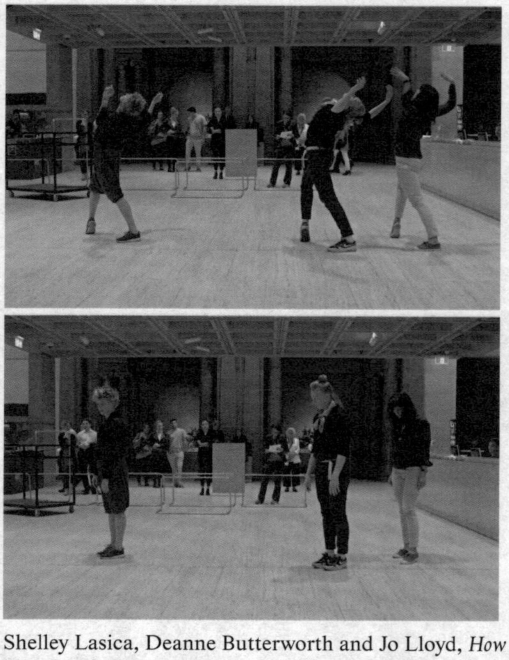

Shelley Lasica, Deanne Butterworth and Jo Lloyd, *How How Choreography Works* 2016, Art Gallery of New South Wales, Sydney, 27 April 2016. Video stills from documentation by Samuel James produced for the 20th Biennale of Sydney

2 — Shelley Lasica is the first Australian dance artist to be represented by a major gallery (City Gallery / Anna Schwartz Gallery, 1989–2006) and has presented her work at the National Gallery of Victoria and Art Gallery of New South Wales, and in various private galleries in Sydney, Melbourne and Cologne (see pp. 657–93). Her role as key artist within the *Precarious Movements: Choreography and the Museum* research project (funded by the Australian Research Council 2021–24) is the result of her unique and longstanding position working across the dance and visual arts communities.

Lineages

In 1968–69, Italian American dance artist Simone Forti was based in Rome and accessed the new Galleria L'Attico as a practice studio outside of opening hours; as she put it, 'no longer accepting my head as my work space, I started using the gallery as my studio'.[3] Using a gallery as a site for dance practice and development was novel at this time. Gallery owner Fabio Sargentini offered an opportunity that was not available in New York, where Forti had previously worked, even though choreographic works were beginning to be presented in galleries and museums there. The commodity-driven economies still attached to New York gallery spaces today made them off-limits for durational artistic development.[4] However, Forti would have been more than comfortable working in a visual arts space, having introduced a new model of cross-artform exchange to the downtown Manhattan art scene after arriving from the West Coast in the early 1960s, a vision of intermediality that chimed with John Cage's 'experimental composition'.[5] Her *Dance Constructions*, which marked her debut in New York, were presented in artist-curated programs in informal gallery contexts.[6] They combined minimal objects, task-based actions, spoken work, improvisation and a pedestrian modality to create a new approach to both composition and dance spectatorship that would influence a generation of choreographers, as well as artists working in other fields.[7]

Forti's role as a mentor, innovator and entrepreneur was the result of an independent course of training in her medium which she began as an adult with contemporary dance pioneer Anna Halprin. Halprin had worked on the West Coast outside the dance establishment as it existed in New York in the 1940s to 1960s, establishing a trans-disciplinary practice engaging with sculpture, dance, theatre, opera and therapy that informed the emerging dance

3 — Julia Bryan-Wilson, 'Simone Forti Goes to the Zoo', *October*, no. 152, Spring 2015, p. 30; and Simone Forti, *Handbook in Motion*, New York University Press, New York, 1974, p. 91.

4 — The Whitney Museum of American Art was a trailblazer in this respect, showing the work of Deborah Hay, Trisha Brown and Yvonne Rainer in their main program in 1969, 1971 and 1970 respectively (Hay's *911 A Dance Concert*, Brown's *Another Fearless Dance Concert* and Rainer's single work, *Continuous Project—Altered Daily*).

5 — The term 'experimental composition' is taken from the title of John Cage's most famous course given at New York's New School where he was a member of the faculty in 1956–61, which was renamed from 'Composition' to 'Experimental Composition' in 1958 (Heather Anderson, 'John Cage', Histories of the New School, 24 Apr 2018, http://newschoolhistories.org/people/john-cage/). Applied to other arts, it refers to the Cagean strategy of repeatedly 'confronting the limits that defined the discipline of composing' of a given art form (Julia Robinson, 'John Cage and Investiture: Unmanning the System', in Julia Robinson (ed.), *The Anarchy of Silence: John Cage and Experimental Art*, Museu d'Art Contemporani de Barcelona, Barcelona, 2009, p. 59).

6 — Forti's *Dance Constructions* were presented across two exhibitions: *Happenings at the Reuben Gallery: Varieties at Reuben Gallery*, New York, 16–18 Dec 1960; and *Five Dance Constructions and Some Other Things, by Simone Morris*, 112 Chambers Street, New York, 26–27 May 1961. The *Dance Constructions* were a landmark acquisition for the Museum of Modern Art in 2016 in terms of museal practices around the art form.

7 — For the influence of Forti and her (female) dance peers on New York–based (male) visual artists working in sculpture, performance and video, see Erin Brannigan, 'Interlude #2: Choreographers and Artists', *Choreography, Visual Art and Experimental Composition 1950s–1970s*, Routledge, London and New York, 2022, pp. 170–84.

Shelley Lasica, *BEHAVIOUR Part 7* 2018, 215 Albion Street, Brunswick, Melbourne, 8 September 2018.
Photos: Jacqui Shelton

avant-garde. Forti's experiences with Halprin, along with her earlier work as a visual artist, resulted in a complete openness to the use of any-material-whatever in her practice, which has spanned painting, sound, sculpture, writing and dance. French dance theorist Laurence Louppe describes how Forti's peer Trisha Brown explored 'dizzyingly unmapped zones' across and between artistic disciplines, becoming an exemplar of 'the rootless freedom of contemporary art'.[8] Brown declares her debt to Forti, as do other colleagues such as Yvonne Rainer, and Forti's unmapping of the contours of the arts at this time was unprecedented. The possibilities she opened up for an expanded contemporary art practice that engaged the emerging field of somatic approaches to dance produced a new field that we might call *dance as contemporary art*.

There are many points of resonation between Forti and Lasica, and Lasica wrote about Forti in 1987, distinguishing her radical innovations from those of the Judson Dance Theater that had eclipsed her legacy for many decades.[9] Lasica's mother, Margaret Lasica, was an original, independent dance artist with initial links to European expressionist dance through training with Elisabet Wiener and Johanna Exiner. She worked in non-theatre spaces and introduced Lasica, as a young choreographer, to a certain self-reflexivity regarding how to frame an audience experience that recalls Forti's work in non-proscenium contexts. Her mother also exposed Lasica to the international dance and theatre avant-garde of the 1970s, specifically a lineage linked to Forti.[10] Early encounters with the work

8 — Laurence Louppe, 'Chaos Made Tangible', in Corinne Diserens (ed.), *Trisha Brown: Danse, précis de liberté*, Musées de Marseille and Réunion des Musées Nationaux, Marseille and Paris, 1998, p. 123.

9 — Shelley Lasica, 'Writing the Past Dance Ideologies', *Writings on Dance*, no. 2, Spring 1987, p. 24. In this article, Lasica raises many issues about the historiography of the 'American postmodernists' that it would takes years for others to arrive at.

10 — Shelley Lasica, interview with the author, 10 Jul 2016.

of Merce Cunningham and Tadeusz Kantor at the Adelaide Festival, in 1976 and 1978 respectively, were pivotal. Her mother also brought out Dana Reitz, a new-generation American choreographer who was working intermedially as a solo artist with light, objects and sound. Lasica came to dance with a mix of other important interests too. She did not study dance in a college or university context but undertook a degree majoring in art history, with an interest in new and alternative presenting frameworks such as Art Projects in Melbourne in the 1970s. Lasica also sought out The Builders Association in New York in the 1990s, Marianne Weems's 'intermedia performance company', to better understand the structures embedded in theatre in its traditional formation.[11]

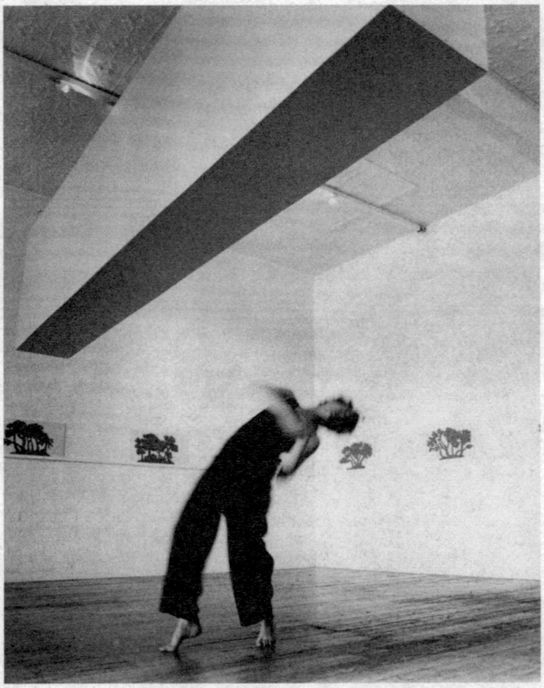

Shelley Lasica, *BELIEVE* 1990–91, City Gallery, Melbourne, 30 November, 1–2 December 1990. Photo: Roger Wood

Back home, Lasica became busy with alternative models of a professional dance community and set up Independent Dance Artists in the late 1980s with Eleanor Brickhill and Felicity MacDonald, with guest artists such as Lucy Guerin and Sandra Parker. It provided a platform for sharing and performing in each other's work outside the funded dance companies in Melbourne. Into the 1990s, her artistic circles took in visual artists and architects, and for an early work like *BELIEVE*, 1990–91, Lasica collaborated with visual artist Tony Clark and architect Roger Wood to make a piece 'about the idea of sculpture, the tussle between the three-dimensional and the two-dimensional; the temporal and the concrete; the intimacy of distance'.[12] This was not work that brought the arts together on stage in 'dialogue', as modelled in the work of Cunningham,

11—Ibid.

12—Shelley Lasica, *TRIPLEX*, 1993, program notes.

but an embodied, choreographic approach to the conditions dance shares with the other arts. In 1994 visual artist Kathy Temin, a friend and colleague who later became a collaborating artist on *CHARACTER X*, 1996, picked up on such tendencies in Lasica's work of the early 1990s:

> Both Robert Morris' feltworks and Eva Hesse's *Area* (1968) share aspects of minimal sculpture but also imply body gestures. To watch Lasica move through space implies sculptural associations. In *Happening* (1992) she angles herself vertically out off the wall while on the floor, so that she resembles a minimal sculpture. Lasica is the body gesturing from the wall in what looks like an elongated stretch. Momentarily Lasica connects both the formal and the physical aspects of being minimal.[13]

Shelley Lasica, *CHARACTER X* 1996, Fitzroy Town Hall, Melbourne, 23 May – 1 June 1996. Photos: Kate Gollings

While Temin's understanding of Lasica's approach to dance referenced the international art canon, Lasica was also embedded in the local context of Melbourne described above. Lasica was busy with work located within a network of influences, colleagues and art forms that was unprecedented in the Australian contemporary dance scene, and she would continue along a path independent of local aesthetic clusters associated with dance theatre, improvisation, butoh/body weather, deconstructed ballet, new media work, dancefilm/installation, and even American postmodern dance.

Radical Independence: The Work of the Work

In the intimate experimental performance scene in Sydney in the 1990s at Performance Space in Redfern, I saw *Square Dance BEHAVIOUR Part 6*, 1996–97, *SITUATION LIVE: THE SUBJECT*, 1997–98, and *DRESS*, 1998 (which had premiered earlier that year at Anna Schwartz Gallery in Melbourne). I later came across the film version of *BEHAVIOUR* (1994) by Margie Medlin when I was programming some dancefilm in the early 2000s. As co-curator of *Scrapbook*

13 — Kathy Temin, 'Untitled', in *Shelley Lasica: Behaviour*, exh. cat., Printed Books, Melbourne, 1994, n.p.

'Live': As Remembered by the Artist, held in September 2011 at Performance Space (an archival project on dance artists with historical connections to that organisation, co-curated with Julie-Anne Long and Mathew Bergan), I worked with Lasica, the only Melbourne artist presented in the program. The movement of choreographers between the two cities was ridiculously rare then, as it continues to be, but Lasica has always had strong connections with Sydney's visual art and performance organisations.

Margie Medlin, *BEHAVIOUR* 1994 (video stills), video based on the solo performance by Shelley Lasica at Store 5, 1993. Courtesy of Shelley Lasica and Margie Medlin

In those early encounters, Lasica's work struck me as being distinct from other dancing happening in Sydney at the time. Its connection to dance practices associated with American mid-century experiments in choreography was a bit familiar. The 'released' quality of dance that presented ease instead of muscular tension, the neutral performance that suspended theatrics, the casual performance context that approached studio-sharing, the reduction of staging to focus on the dancing body—all of these I had encountered in the work of Sydney-based artists such as Russell Dumas, Rosalind Crisp, Sue-Ellen Kohler and Eleanor Brickhill, and Melbourne-based Ros Warby, Trevor Patrick, Sandra Parker and Lucy Guerin (fresh back from New York), all Lasica's peers. But there was something else at play that was as intriguing as it was elusive. The difference between what Lasica was doing and everything else was impossible for me to pinpoint at the time, and I never wrote about Lasica's work during this period.

Shelley Lasica with Martin Grant, *DRESS* 1998, Anna Schwartz Gallery, Melbourne, 12–15 February 1998. Photos: Kate Gollings

Lasica was reconfiguring the disciplinary parameters of the art form, and I lacked a map for the new terrain she was venturing into. Thinking about *DRESS* now, I recall Lasica making her way slowly into the space, framed by her audience eased up against the four walls in silent attention (there was no sound score, as in much of her work of this period). I remember thinking that her movement had a self-conscious grace, softness and delicacy that wasn't very common in other dance work at the time. She was performing femininity and performing dress, the other star of the show. Lasica's room notes describe how 'the outfit both defines and resists the performance of it', and I recall it making a brief appearance with undergarments and nudity, like a rare and precious thing that might overwhelm the whole if it had too much exposure.[14] The dress, designed by Martin Grant using reassembled historical garments, was in duet with Lasica, and my reductive interpretation circled around gesture and identity, restraint and detail, and behaviour and form.

Shelley Lasica with Martin Grant, *DRESS* 1998, Anna Schwartz Gallery, Melbourne, 15 February 1998. Video stills from documentation by Roger Wood

I cheat on my memory exercise (the dance critic's mode) and look at the Anna Schwartz Gallery video documentation from the same year. It's a discrete single shot, from the floor in a corner. Hand, arm and hip behaviours strike me as signatures: softly held fingers on carefully placed wrists; arms held off the body and giving form to the space around Lasica like a voluminous garment; hips jaunting to throw the whole body into a shape, everything else falling into place around; and pacing—Lasica rarely rushes. It makes me feel sentimental. Even now, despite her large casts in recent works, when I think of Lasica's art I

14 — Shelley Lasica, *DRESS*, 1998, program notes.

still think of her solo, tentatively feeling her way into a room where people wait in anticipation of proximity, a certain coolness, a sharp perceptiveness despite her soft gaze, a casual yet disciplined choreography.

These details of the dancing were the things I could access easily at the time. As Temin notes, 'she is not controversial in what she actually does'.[15] But it was everything framing the movement that indicated that something else was going on, something new to me. The status of the body (as subject–object), the way the movements were proffered to my gaze, and the contingency of an attentive presence attuned to the specific moment all appeared as things that could constitute the content of the work in and of itself. The tentative, casual attitude in performance gestured towards both the body–object and the everyday body. The body and its movements were presented to my gaze from a distance, not within an emotionally invested or spectacular economy, but not without sensitivity and care. And the proximity to the dancer's perceptual activity and associated disciplined physical work that tuned itself to the room exposed the work of the work in a new way; as something unique to this present, yet indebted to a continuity of iterations-as-practice.

Lasica meets the other arts in the 'trans' of trans-discipline—the exchange with other media registers at the level of the dancing body, not as an arbitrary link between the dancer and other scenographic elements, nor under a ruling order (story, character, theme) that directs various media under its service. Detached from explicit, externally sourced content, the physical activity thus exposed can be put into dialogue with any number of things associated with and dependent upon the dancer dancing. With no language-based equivalents for Shelley Lasica's work, the choreographies open onto multiple (often critical) relations with extra-disciplinary material that is expansive and inclusive of other media, contextual parameters, conditions of operation, political resonances, philosophical work and social imperatives.

Of course, every work of art is experienced within a network of relations, but there is something *explicit* about this focus in Lasica's work (a sharp sense that there is much more going on here than qualities of movement and their composition) which is combined with *implicit* intermediality, contextual critique and socio-political commentary (you need to attend to the dancing to access its subtly significant positioning).

These aspects of Lasica's work connect with some important elements in the contemporary arts that theorist Peter Osborne has identified in his account of the 'postconceptual': art which is trans-disciplinary and telescopic; temporally expansive and unhinged from specific iterations; yet deeply self-aware of the contemporaneous context, institutional frames and debts to the past.[16] Lasica often works in a series structure and cross-references her oeuvre across its full historical extent, insisting on the contingent and continuous nature of the whole. Her institutional critique carefully considers how, where and why work appears in the public domain; she has noted that choreography is not reducible

15—Temin, 'Untitled', n.p.

16—Peter Osborne, *Anywhere or Not at All: Philosophy of Contemporary Art*, Verso, London, 2013, p. 43.

to performance, which is only one part of an expanded and ongoing practice.[17] These are the terms on which Lasica engages with the contemporary or current state of the arts.

Form and Behaviour

Influential German theatre scholar Hans-Thies Lehmann (whose model of 'post-dramatic theatre' I always thought owed much to contemporary dance) has written that 'form and behaviour' can sometimes take the place of 'meaning' in performance.[18] *BEHAVIOUR* is the title of one of Lasica's choreographic series, with iterations across 1993–2018. Other works are called *Happening Simultaneously*, 1991, *SITUATION LIVE: THE SUBJECT*, 1997–98 (part of the *Situation* series), *Something Happens*, 2010, and *AS WE MAKE IT*, 2016. As these titles suggest, and as discussed above, one of the primary things we are watching when we are part of an audience for Lasica's work is people displaying behaviours and attitudes, connecting, reacting, creating 'happenings' and 'makings' live in an intimate space which highlights the co-presence of performers and audience. Through 'various systems of generating material and performing in that space between set material and improvisation', Lasica keeps the awareness of co-presence alive and vital in performance.[19]

Rehearsal images, Shelley Lasica, *Here BEHAVIOUR Part 4* 1995. Photos: Kate Gollings

But what do those behaviours consist of within a given work? What *form* do they take? Lasica says little of this but there may be a clue in her 'Retrospective' article for *Brolga* that echoes Temin: 'it is not that the material is extraordinary in itself, it is rather that in approaching it in a certain way, it seems as if the process can offer certain possibilities—the way I can understand and work with it in my own body, and with the other dancers'.[20] While the movement material might be of less concern than how it is embodied across various dancers, or across various works in new relationships and contexts, there is no doubt that Lasica's movement language has qualities, intentions and characteristics that constitute, for want of a better word, a 'style'. In ensemble works such as *Solos*

17 — Erin Brannigan, 'Context, Discipline, and Understanding: The Poetics of Shelley Lasica's Gallery-Based Work', *Performance Paradigm*, vol. 13, 2016, pp. 107–08, https://www.performanceparadigm.net/index.php/journal/article/view/196/193.
18 — Hans-Thies Lehmann, 'Excess of Time: Some Remarks on Durational Aesthetics', in Barbara Grounau, Matthias von Hartz and Carolin Hochleichter (eds), *How to Frame: On the Threshold of Performing and Visual Arts*, Sternberg Press, Berlin, 2016, p. 78.
19 — Lasica, *TRIPLEX*, program notes.
20 — Shelley Lasica, 'Retrospective', *Brolga*, no. 33, Dec 2010, p. 24.

for Other People, 2015, *The Design Plot*, 2017–, or *How How Choreography Works*, 2016, we see movements ricochet from the past across multiple bodies, citations linking past to present, and familiarity connecting communities of dancers across generations. Lasica notes, 'it is because my practice has been so influenced by working as a solo performer [for around ten years], that relationship to a personal lexicon is very strong for me'.[21] How form can be apprehended in the work is then cumulative for her audiences; it consists of certain gestures, postures, rhythms, patterns and repetitions, and in group work it occurs as specific groupings in space–time and the way flurries of energy and stasis are juxtaposed to (re)create familiar rhythms. Her use of form is also 'characteristically multi-focal, calling for a diffused spectatorship: there are always multiple points of interest'.[22]

In the solo at Performance Space, *Square Dance BEHAVIOUR Part 6*, 1996–97, and Medlin's film version *BEHAVIOUR*, 1994, I recall dancing that worked the space between behaviour and form; 'between the medium of dance, the theatrical body, and the audiences [*sic*] expectations'.[23] A discursive approach to the relationship between these things is the primary content of the work, and Lasica has spoken elsewhere about instructions for her dancers related to the 'physical, emotional and theoretical space between people'.[24] Watching a documentation VHS tape of three performances of *BEHAVIOUR* at Store 5 in Prahran in 1993, I recall the dancing that shares many of the characteristics mentioned above: slow and dramatic arm and hand gestures that frame the moving body as if amplifying it, thrusting hips leading the body along, sudden weight drops into the pelvis or knees. Lasica is bold, holding the centre of the room or moving into the onlookers' space, then striking out in a new direction with loping steps. This movement is compelling. But in the last recorded version, which is performed without an audience in the sharp afternoon, it's not *the work* I see. The movements alone are not the work; the audience completes it.

Through her dancing, Lasica puts forces, attitudes and power relations into play between herself, the movement material and the audience. In the simple act of looking back at those who gaze upon her in the proximity of the small storeroom, identified by Temin as a choreographic strategy in *BEHAVIOUR Part 1*, Lasica efficiently hones everyone's attention to what is happening between dancing, the dancer and the onlooker in the space. As Temin also notes, there is a lack of 'task'—so common to performance art and a characteristic of many dance works for the gallery. The compositional logic is not on the surface of the work but is embodied and multi-dimensional.[25] The audience does not get a 'free ride' by easily deducing a plan of action that drives the apparatus along, taking our attention away from the action/behaviour/situation/happening. Lasica herself has described the focus on 'the presentness of physical actions' and beyond her early solos, as she has invited other dancers into her work, this

21 — Ibid.
22 — Shelley Lasica, *ACTION SITUATION*, 1999, program notes.
23 — Shelley Lasica and Margie Medlin, 'Behaviour video text, 1995', unpublished.
24 — Lasica, interview, 2016.
25 — Temin, 'Untitled', n.p.

focus has turned more and more to the relationship *between the dancers*.[26] This approach is in sync with American choreographer Jennifer Lacey's description of contemporary dance as being about 'people spending time together, thinking by behaving, and modify[ing] their thoughts by modifying their behavior'.[27] We are watching a social situation when we watch Lasica's ensemble work.

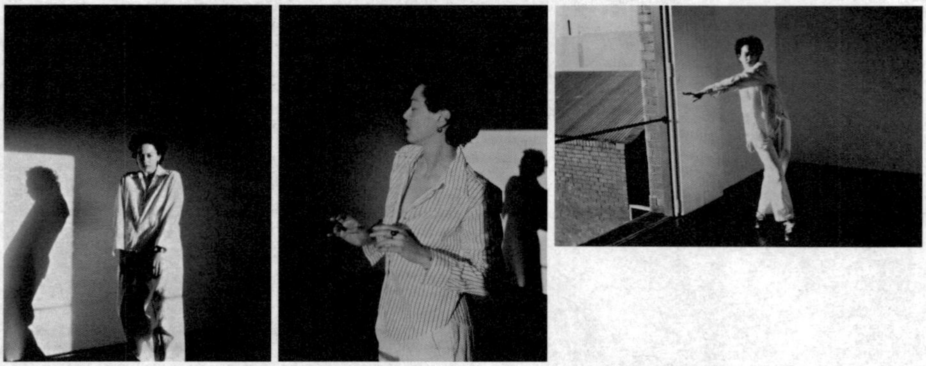

Shelley Lasica, *BEHAVIOUR Part 1* 1993, Store 5, Melbourne, 24–28 November 1993. Photos: Roger Wood

* * *

I opened with Lasica alone in the Art Gallery of New South Wales foyer in Sydney recalling Forti dancing alone in a gallery space as studio in Rome nearly half a century earlier ... there is something about solo practice that allows for the leap into new terrain that Lasica has undertaken, following the lead of other radical artists.[28] Lasica's sustained choice to interrogate the frameworks of where, how and when dance happens has placed her as independent of national dance infrastructures and proximal to the institutional critique spearheaded by conceptual art. One could argue that the emergence of conceptual art in the work of neo-Dada, Fluxus and minimal artists such as Robert Rauschenberg, La Monte Young, Sol LeWitt and Robert Morris is unthinkable without the influence of Cunningham, Halprin, Rainer and Forti. And here stands Lasica in the foyer of the Art Gallery of New South Wales, sizing up the museum with her diminutive presence and subtle gestures. What has been a 'minor' history is making its legacy increasingly clear, and the thing called choreography ('that is not a thing') will make its presence felt through the persistence of dance artists like Lasica.

26— Lasica, *ACTION SITUATION*, program notes.
27— Jennifer Lacey, 'Jennifer Lacey in Conversation with Mathieu Copeland Gare de l'Est, Paris, 16 October 2010', in Mathieu Copeland and Julie Pellegrin (eds), *Choreographing Exhibitions*, Les presses du réel, Dijon, 2013, p. 127. Lasica, Lloyd and Butterworth articulate a similar sentiment: 'Choreography can take on multiple forms and is porous and mutable, but resides so intrinsically in how we think socially'. (Shelley Lasica, Jo Lloyd and Deanne Butterworth, 'Shelley Lasica in Conversation with Jo Lloyd and Deanne Butterworth', in *How Choreography Works*, exh. cat., West Space, Melbourne, 2015, n.p.).
28— Lasica refers to the solo mode as 'a research model' and 'discipline' (Lasica, interview, 2016).

Shelley Lasica: Body of Work
Robyn McKenzie

In the early 1990s I started taking Margaret Lasica's classes in the Orr Street studio 'Extensions' in Carlton. Although at the end of each class we did join sequences of movement together, I hesitate to call them dance classes. The focus was not on learning and reproducing a set repertoire of movements, but more on first principles—exploring how the body moves and understanding the capacity and the limits of that movement.[1] Around the same time I started going to Shelley Lasica's performances.

I saw each reflected in the other: mother and daughter. Margaret's classes were like 'notes towards' a type of contemporary dance that Shelley's performances exemplified. Margaret Lasica (1926–1993) was a pioneer of modern dance in Australia. She founded the Modern Dance Ensemble in Melbourne in 1967—which continued as a performing group through the 1970s, disbanding in 1981—after which she focused on teaching.[2] This was the modern dance Shelley grew up with, through which she first learned how to be a dancer.

While there is a lot that came to distinguish mother and daughter in terms of attitudes to dance performance and professional practice, they shared a basic approach to the use of the body. It was a conception of dance as a movement language, based on the body's given attributes or allowances: propensities of joints and limbs, their rotations around each other, how they flex and bend, their physical extension and countervailing retreats; forces of lift followed by fall and flop, of expansion and contraction, coil and leap.

I keep wanting to use the term 'natural' to describe this type of movement—to distinguish it from the unnatural postures and over-extension of the body found in ballet, for example, such as standing *en pointe*. This dance draws closer to the body of the everyday and its motivations—gesture, expression and social patterning: running for the bus, standing in line, playing with the dog and, indeed, dancing. But natural? No. It trains the body. It has history.

On Tuesdays at the Orr Street studio there was a class before mine, and there was a period for the crossover when people in that class were packing up and leaving and our new class was settling in, putting our mats down on the floor, doing some stretches perhaps. Margaret habitually called the class to order, signaling it was time to start, with the words (approximate): 'OK, it's time to do some work now.'

* * *

1—Rachel Fensham interviewing Shelley and Wendy Lasica, 'Studio practices 1, extensions: room to move', *RealTime*, no. 9, Oct–Nov 1995, p. 36, accessed 4 Mar 2022, http://www.realtimearts.net/article/9/10081. Speaking of Extensions, the Carlton studio that Margaret Lasica opened in 1980, Shelley says: 'In the last few years, Margaret became less interested in teaching vocational classes and more in teaching people who just wanted to move, to find out about their bodies and extend their functional use.'

2—After 1981 the Ensemble continued to produce occasional works. Ann Standish, entry on Margaret Lasica in *The Encyclopedia of Women & Leadership in Twentieth-Century Australia*, accessed 4 Mar 2022, https://www.womenaustralia.info/leaders/biogs/WLE0232b.htm.

Margaret Lasica amassed a significant library which had its own room in the Lasica home.[3] It included titles on visual art, philosophy, dance, music and theatre, and was accompanied by a comprehensive record collection: from the Strasbourg Percussion Ensemble to Osibisa. Collated during a period of expansive thinking about the body, movement and performance, this library made it possible to read about Wilhelm Reich and his concept of the armoured body alongside local takes on the feminist body in *LIP* magazine. As well as monthly editions of *Artforum* you could find almost a full run of Richard Schechner's *The Drama Review*, with its focus on experimental, avant-garde, interdisciplinary performance. This was also part of the context that Shelley Lasica grew up in, and that influenced her ideas about what dance could be.

Through the 1980s crossover activity between the visual arts, music, fashion and architecture was a defining characteristic of Melbourne's creative scene. Lasica, then studying for an arts degree at Melbourne University, was part of this world. She was a fit model for young fashion designers Martin Grant and Fiona Scanlan and did runway modelling for a number of designers in the Fashion Design Council's annual parades at the Palais Theatre in St Kilda.[4] On campus, she volunteered at the Ewing and George Paton Galleries, a hub of activity and new ideas. Post-structuralist thought was influential among the student cohort. Paul Taylor was publishing *Art & Text* out of Victoria College in Prahran. After graduating with a major in Fine Arts (Art History), Lasica worked as an assistant to commercial gallerist Christine Abrahams.

From the outset Lasica understood her work in the context of an interdisciplinary, experimental art world, rather than a medium-specific dance world. She positioned her work by choosing to perform in gallery spaces and to work in collaboration with visual artists, architects and other designers.

In 1990 Lasica's solo performance *BELIEVE* debuted at City Gallery in Melbourne, a commercial gallery space at 45 Flinders Lane. For this performance Shelley invited architect Roger Wood (her then partner) and artist Tony Clark to collaborate on the design of the performance space or mise-en-scène. Roger Wood designed a group of three sculptural volumes: a rectangular form painted yellow-gold that was suspended from the ceiling on an angle, hung above head-height in the middle of the performance space; another painted pink that looked like a cantilever extending from the back wall; and a third black volume, also suspended. On a series of 10 by 15 inch canvas boards Tony Clark created a frieze of trees painted in a poppingly bright combination of greens on a blue background. It ran along the floor on the long side wall of the gallery, forming the backdrop to the performance area.

The gallery was at basement level in an old building, and was painted white throughout, including the structural iron pillars that ran down the centre

3 — Margaret Lasica's library was donated to the Victorian College of the Arts Library, University of Melbourne.

4 — Lasica wore designs by Grant and Scanlan in a standalone, solo performance at Reconnaissance Gallery in 1986: *Describing the perspective of time, It promises you nothing*, Reconnaissance Gallery, Fitzroy, 5–7 Sep 1986. She worked again with Grant, collaborating over a two-year period in the development of the performance *DRESS*, presented by Anna Schwartz Gallery in association with the Woolmark Fashion Festival in 1998.

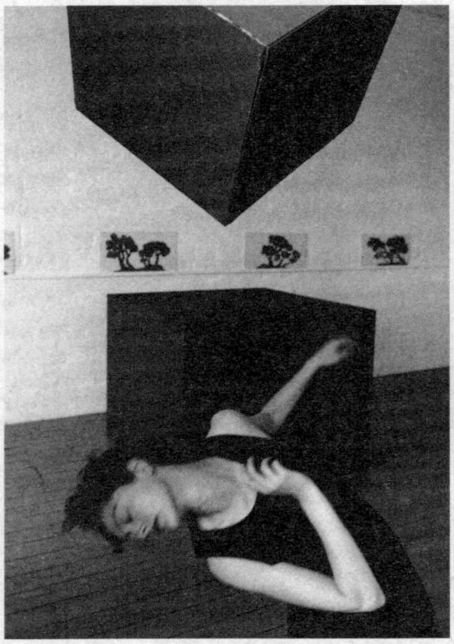

Shelley Lasica, *BELIEVE* 1990–91. Left: City Gallery, Melbourne, 30 November, 1–2 December 1990. Right: Yuill|Crowley Gallery, Sydney, 19–21 February 1991. Photos: Roger Wood

of the room. The effect of this 'white-out' was to dissolve spatial coordinates. The material interventions made by Wood and Clark in the white non-space of the gallery created reference points, reinstating a spatial ground against which Lasica's movement could be seen. They introduced scale, dimension, form and colour, all of which her movements necessarily interacted with, by dint of being in the same space at the same time. The nature of this collaboration between architecture, painting and dance was confined here to a literal 'coming together' through co-existence within the space, but otherwise each remained separate and independent.

Shelley Lasica, *BEHAVIOUR Part 1* 1993, Store 5, Melbourne, 24–28 November 1993. Photos: Roger Wood

The performance I remember most vividly from those early years was another solo work: *BEHAVIOUR Part 1*, presented at Store 5 in 1993. Store 5 was an artist-run initiative, a small exhibition space accessed from the end of a cobbled laneway off High Street in Prahran, near the corner of Chapel Street. From early 1989 it ran a program of one-day exhibitions, open on Saturday afternoons.

The size of Store 5, a room approximately three-and-a-half metres wide and six metres deep, determined much about it as an exhibition venue, and the nature of the viewing experience. There was a performance element to visiting exhibitions at Store 5—as I have written elsewhere, 'it made "looking at art" a form of ritual theatre'. When visiting, 'the physical set-up meant that you felt your viewing experience/practice was as much on display as the works in the exhibition itself: you were conscious of how much time you spent, what you actually looked at and how.'[5]

Lasica's performance exploited this aspect of the space, using the intimacy of its dimensions to make the 'behaviour of viewing' part of the work. As an audience member in the small space of Store 5, lining up with others against the walls waiting for the performance to begin, you were intensely aware of yourself in the space—of where and how you were standing, your mien or attitude, and your interactions with others. Lasica was in the space also, standing, talking. Something in her stance, her behaviour changed or shifted. Silence. With the audience arrayed around all sides, forming part of the mise-en-scène or backdrop, the distinction between artist and spectator, performer and audience, exhibition and looking, dance and ordinary everyday movement is blurred. Her performance had begun, our performance continued.

These two works, *BELIEVE* and *BEHAVIOUR Part 1*, took place in two very different gallery contexts, in terms of physical space and organisational model. The first of these factors, the physical space, has an obvious role, and in a sense, can be seen as a collaborative partner; the organisational or institutional framework also has effects—creating context, and determining audience. In this sense also, spaces can be seen as a collaborative partner. The request to use City Gallery for the performance of *BELIEVE* initiated a professional relationship with co-director Anna Schwartz that led to Lasica later being represented by the eponymously named Anna Schwartz Gallery (opened in 1993). This association was important for Lasica in defining her professional identity and a context for her work. Lasica would have been the only dance practitioner represented by a commercial gallery in Australia at that time. The relationship was unique both for the gallery and its director, and for Lasica.

* * *

In the later 1990s Lasica expanded her practice as a choreographer in a series of ensemble works of increasing complexity, involving an increasing number of performers and co-contributors. Jo Lloyd and Deanne Butterworth first danced together for Lasica in *SITUATION LIVE: THE SUBJECT*, 1997–98. They were joined in *ACTION SITUATION*, 1999, by a third dancer, Kylie Walters (for the Melbourne performances), and in *History Situation*, 2002, there were five dancers. While there were other works in the sequence, these three built on one another.[6]

5—Robyn McKenzie, 'The Local Group: Store 5 1989–1993', in Max Delany (ed.), *Pitch Your Own Tent*, Monash University Gallery, Clayton, Vic., Jul 2005, p. 38.
6—There were further works in the larger *Situation* series made during these years: *live drama situation*, Cleveland, London, 27 May 1997; *LIVE OPERA SITUATION*, Wesleyan Hall, Albert Park, 15–18, 21–25 Jul 1998; *RESTRICTED SITUATION* (with a video by Callum Morton), Revolver, Melbourne, 22–25 Sep 1999.

Lasica was director as well as choreographer for the three productions. She did not herself perform. While recognisably works by Shelley Lasica, they derived from a set of co-creative relationships, the nature of which varied according to the individuals she worked with, as determined in part by the jobs they were doing, and as the relationships developed over time. I know this from first-hand experience, as the writer of 'source scripts' that were commissioned for each of the three works.

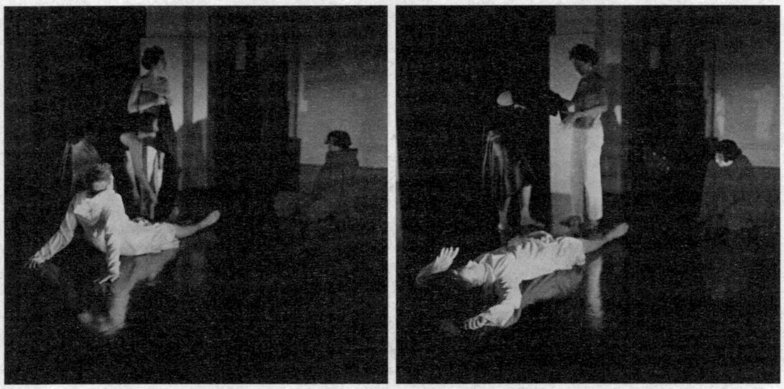

Rehearsal images, Shelley Lasica, *ACTION SITUATION* 1999, East Wing Gallery, Immigration Museum, Melbourne, 12–14, 18–20 February 1999. Pictured: Jo Lloyd, Kylie Walters, Shelley Lasica and Deanne Butterworth.

I had written on contemporary art for local art magazines since the mid 1980s and from the mid 1990s was art critic on the *Age* newspaper.[7] I was not a creative writer. When Shelley asked me to collaborate, it was an intriguing proposal. I was to write a script for a contemporary dance performance, but the performance would not be an interpretation of the text (the script), rather the script was going to be one element used to create the performance. The script would not be a 'story' summarised in program notes that is 'acted out' by the dancers. It would work behind the scenes, hence 'source script'. In 'readings' with the dancers followed by improvisation sessions the script was to be used to

Publicity image, Shelley Lasica, *SITUATION LIVE: THE SUBJECT* 1997–98. Pictured: Deanne Butterworth and Jo Lloyd. Photo: Kate Gollings

7—When Louise Adler became arts editor in 1995, she appointed two writers for each art form. Robert Nelson and I were the writers for the visual arts.

generate a movement vocabulary and syntax. Perhaps they would draw on the dynamics of the relationships between characters in the script and the emotional colour of their interactions or rhythms of speech, or analyse their actions following the sequencing of scenes/locations/times.

The freedom of the task was demanding in terms of thinking through the options it allowed, and the possibilities for experiment. For my first script for *SITUATION LIVE,* I chose a 'kitchen sink drama'—two protagonists, minimal physical action, and only a little more dialogue. *ACTION SITUATION* (the second in the series) in contrast, had a grand landscape setting with lots of physical action (including seismic activity and a landslide), and even bigger and more volatile emotions. For *History Situation*, I played more with the form of the writing itself: constructing the action around a theatre set and ensemble cast, while writing the script with directions for cinema. In each case, as the work built up and more layers were added to it—through musical score/sound, lighting design and costuming as well as through the development of the choreography—the legibility of the text as a narrative source would recede. Lasica's choreography was not, in any case, linear. Actions were multiple and simultaneous, and it was up to the viewer to decide on their focus, to choose what at any moment was of primary interest and thus construct their own viewing experience and reading of the event.

Although diffused in this way, the point of interest in the experiment was to see what would survive through this process. What opportunities would be presented through this intervention, 'the tension between the illusionistic space and time of narrative, and the "presentness" of physical actions unfolding through real time and space in performance'?[8] These works were thought of by Lasica as being in dialogue with theatre, and were staged in theatrical venues where possible, beginning with *SITUATION LIVE* at the iconic La Mama in Carlton. *History Situation* was held at Horti Hall, originally built by the Victorian Horticultural Improvement Society and then, as now, the home of Opera Victoria.

Lasica's instructions to me were minimal. She usually does not have a pre-determined idea of what a person may do. Rather, collaborators are asked to contribute something from those parts or aspects of their practice that, as identified by Lasica, 'make an interesting conversation' with her interests.[9] Some collaborative relationships are longstanding: she had worked with composer François (Franc) Tétaz and lighting specialist John Ford a number of times before *SITUATION LIVE*. The collaboration with costume maker Shio Otani was new. This was an area Lasica was confident working in, and the relationship with her collaborators was more often a working partnership. Margaret Lasica had trained as a pattern maker—her day job before she married. In habitual forays into the city that were more about looking at clothes than shopping for them, Shelley gleaned from Margaret a knowledge of fabrics and their behaviour, the relationship of cut to the moving body, and the consequent fall or line of clothing.

In the *Situation* series the costuming of the dancers reinforced the composition of each ensemble, and its dynamics. In *SITUATION LIVE*, Shio

8—*ACTION SITUATION*, program notes, Melbourne, Feb 1999.

9—Shelley Lasica, in conversation with the author, 5 Mar 2022.

Otani dressed the two dancers in top and skirt of contrasting geometric and floral designs, in the reverse combination to each other. The interaction of the two dancers set in motion a dynamic play reminiscent of Russian constructivist experiments: a competing dualism that was complex and nuanced. The colour blocking of the dancers in *ACTION SITUATION* in black, white and red costumes established the idea of three clearly individuated elemental identities. By contrast, all the dancers in *History Situation* wore a similar uniform: they acted as a group. Working on the costumes for *ACTION SITUATION* with designer/maker Kara Baker led to a ten-year collaboration on a clothing label titled Project. The first range they produced was based on the hooded cagoule tops with paired skirts and pants first developed for the performance. Richard

Shelley Lasica, *VIANNE* 2008–09, fortyfivedownstairs, Melbourne, 3–14 December 2008.
Pictured: Deanne Butterworth, Jo Lloyd and Bonnie Paskas. Photos: Rohan Young

Nylon, who worked on the costumes for *History Situation*, collaborated again with Lasica on her contribution to Fiona Macdonald's *Museum Emotions*, 2003.[10]

VIANNE was first staged in 2008 in the same physical space as the 1990 solo *BELIEVE* (now the gallery, theatre and performance space fortyfivedownstairs), with an ensemble cast of five and with collaborating artist Anne-Marie May, known for her dynamic spatial constructions. In 2012, after a four-year gap, the collaboration was renegotiated to present *VIANNE AGAIN* at three separate venues in Melbourne. As part of the presentation at Monash Art, Design and Architecture, Lasica invited artist Helen Grogan to make a new work. Grogan's *INSIDE THURSDAY—VIANNE AGAIN (Drawing Room D112, MADA)*, 2012, an installation and online work, was made in close conversation with Lasica to sit alongside *VIANNE AGAIN*. Grogan, Lasica and May then collaborated on *INSIDE VIANNE AGAIN (National Gallery of Victoria)* for presentation in Melbourne Now at the NGV in 2013–14. This final iteration comprised a dual-channel video of visual and audio material from *VIANNE* that was performed and shot in the same gallery space it would be exhibited in. The installation, which included new three-dimensional works by Anne-Marie May, took up a corner of the exhibition space, with the video projected straight onto the wall. It seems to me this work has a metaphorical side. Each iteration of *VIANNE* required Lasica to renegotiate with her collaborators, as well as with the social, institutional and financial structures that support making dance.

On occasion the shoe has been on the other foot, with Lasica commissioned to perform in works by other artists, as in *Represent* with Tony Clark, a work which has now gone through five iterations: including the original at Galerie Seippel in Cologne in 2013. It was performed again at Murray White Room in Melbourne in March 2014; in the Cork Forest at the National Arboretum in Canberra in December that year; in front of a select audience in a domestic interior in Militello, Sicily; and lastly at 11m2, a gallery in Berlin, in 2018.

Represent is a riff on the famous Portland Vase—a Roman glass cameo vase that in 1790 Josiah Wedgwood duplicated in a production-ware edition of his ceramic jasperware.[11] Around the vase are seven figures that divide into two distinct scenes, the interpretation of which remains a matter of debate. Landscape provides a background matrix that supports the figure compositions: a tree here, a rocky outcrop there. In *Represent*, Lasica rotates through the figure poses on the vase with Clark's painted landscape on a canvas backdrop as support (Clark painted a new canvas backdrop for each iteration.) In this contemporary re-imagining, figure and ground are divided between the four-dimensional reality in space and time of Lasica's performance and Clark's two-dimensional painted backdrop. Lasica plays with this relationship: at one point while seated on the ground, for example, she props an elbow on a painted

10 — Lasica was the choreographer for artist Fiona Macdonald's 'conceptual soap opera' *Museum Emotions*, 2003. This 104-minute video and 'contemporary art story' features a cast of Melbourne art-world figures, as well as dancers Deanne Butterworth, Jacob Lehrer and Jo Lloyd.

11 — Tony Clark has had a longstanding interest in Wedgwood's jasperware as representing an iconic moment in art history when the classical tradition meets popular culture.

rocky outcrop for support as she leans back in the pose of the figure commonly identified as 'Ariadne languishing on Naxos'.

The most important of Lasica's co-creative relationships is with her dancers, who characteristically work intensively with Lasica on a project in a series of staged development and rehearsal programs. The distinctive energies and ways of moving of her dancers are not just allowed expression in Lasica's choreography but are also harnessed and celebrated. She has had a particularly long and fruitful engagement with Deanne Butterworth and Jo Lloyd. Both dancers are kinaesthetically distinctive in physical movement styles of seemingly opposed character, and entirely complementary.

Rehearsal images, Shelley Lasica, *WHEN I AM NOT THERE* 2022, Princes Park, Melbourne, 27 October 2021. Photos: Jacqui Shelton

Preparation of new work planned to accompany this exhibition was affected by the COVID-19 pandemic and restrictions on social gathering. This circumstance led to the opening up of another avenue for research and development—a shared reading program. Like many artists, during this time Lasica and her collaborators found new ways to work together. Lasica started off by sharing the things she had read in her preparation for the current work. She had organised architect Colby Vexler and artist/writer Lisa Radford to take part in the development process as 'consultants', together with her long-term collaborator, composer Franc Tétaz, and the dancers. The state's COVID-19 restrictions set the parameters by which the group could interact. Those who lived within five kilometres of each other could meet to walk, talk and dance together. Scans and voice recordings of readings were shared and commented on via Dropbox. The group met using Zoom. In response to these conversations the dancers suggested further readings to the group, moving the dialogue forwards. There were phone conversations, books sent, and comments returned by mail.

* * *

Lasica continues to experiment with ways of making dance. Her network of collaborators has been impressive in its cross-disciplinary breadth, from sound artists and composers, lighting designers, film and video makers, who as part of their professional identity might work in an applied way, to artists, architects, fashion designers and writers more used to their creative autonomy. Her relationships have been based on specific conversations she has had with individuals, which are different to those she has had with other people. These relationships do not construct a shared space or constitute a milieu. It has never been a requirement of the relationship between Lasica and her collaborators that there be an understanding or agreement about a project and where it might be heading. As with *BELIEVE*, individual contributions can and did remain separate and independent. Lasica's methodology does not require a shared aesthetic understanding. The invitation to collaborate is not predicated on a compounding effect—the idea that the resultant work will, as the saying goes, be more than the sum of its parts.

Lasica does not belong to one group but drops in and out of many. She has a network of connections. These relationships of connection are not just between creative practices or disciplines, but between people and the different spaces in the city where they come together, and the different histories and regimes of sociality that govern those spaces. Her work has been to choreograph this network.

Among and Against: Lasica's Contacts

Justin Clemens

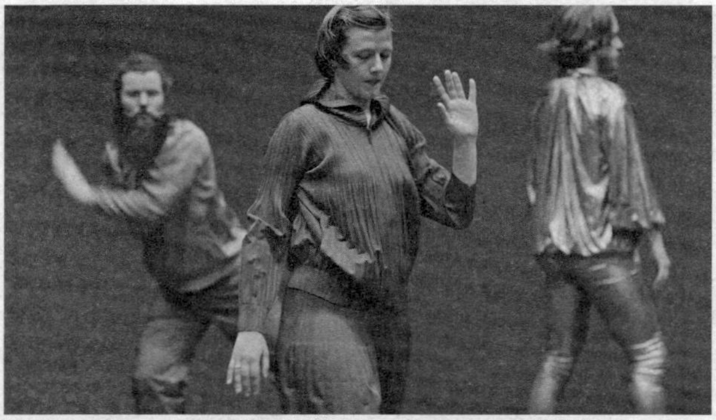

Shelley Lasica, *The Design Plot* 2017 (video stills), video from the performance staged at the Royal Melbourne Tennis Club, Melbourne, 2017. Pictured: Daniel Newell, Ellen Davies and Timothy Harvey (top); Ellen Davies and Lilian Steiner (above). Director: James Wright

They stride rapidly onto the royal (or 'real') tennis court in single file, faces set, focused, in striking clothes in bright colours and strict designs—sharp blue, geometrical and harlequinade, gold lamé, pixelated—disposing themselves in postures at once odd and everyday. Fragments of poses and movements emerge, this one yogic, that one balletic, the six figures moving at once monadically—windowlessly, as the German polymath Gottfried Leibniz might have said—entirely caught in their own routine, swivelling and shifting in their own rhythms, yet also seemingly in accord with an enigmatic preformation of the whole. The court's floor is gridded; the walls a peculiar pseudo-medieval green; the closely reticulated net divides the space and the dancers. The wall's green is further decorated with the insignia of the king's crown and a crude image of a tonsured monk. Every now and again the bodies encounter each other directly: is that an embrace? a gesture of defiance or abnegation, enjoyment or resignation? aiding and abetting? assault and battery? the testing of an irreality? And every now and again, a transient coordination. A foot rubs a back, or a hand pushes away a head. The faces themselves are part of the performance, fringed with hair, impassive, decided, decisive, uncertain. You can hear the dancers' sneakers squeaking and squealing as they shift about the space.

A woman in black lies on her back on the parquet floor of a gallery, one leg perpendicular in the air. Suddenly she swings to her feet and leaps up, leaving the floor altogether. She swings her arms rapidly in front, bends and spins, stops momentarily, takes several quick steps forward, her body bending very slightly back as her arms open like the wings of a kung-fu crane, her right leg bent and the foot turned wide out. Halt. Pulse. A very slow shake, then a couple of surprising sideways hops, arms moving outwards until the body bends again and the arms make a gesture of expulsion or dismissal. Another twist. A step. A stop.

Shelley Lasica (pictured), Deanne Butterworth and Jo Lloyd, *How Choreography Works* 2015, West Space, Melbourne, 9 October, 24 October, 6–7 November 2015. Photos: Christo Crocker

The same woman, again in a black singlet, stands among a crowd in a long gallery with white walls and concrete floors. The crowd is rowdy, restless. A hush. The woman reaches up into the air, turns around, and then begins to step peculiarly across the floor, her rear leg moving heel first to propel her forward, her hands rolling in deep soft waves; after a few of these odd steps, she gives a sudden high kick that folds to a pithy, controlled stagger, and then to an almost indolent halt. She lifts her arms and her right leg in the air, briefly becoming a dark star as the leg coils behind her back and around while her whole body slowly gyres and sinks to the floor in a controlled slump. She totters and flails, somehow gracefully slows into a kind of tableau vivant of classical statuary, pivots again, steps forwards, backwards, clearing a space into which another woman, also in black, suddenly lunges, hunched and spasmodic, making jerky little steps that take her forwards and backwards in a little space, utterly different in shape and effect to the first dancer, who continues to sway and swing to her own rhythm.

Shelley Lasica and Deanne Butterworth, *DUELLE* 2009, Centre for Contemporary Photography, Melbourne, 18 December 2009. Photos: Terence Hogan

These are all descriptions—or rather indications—of fragments of iterations of works by Shelley Lasica, in which she also performs: *The Design Plot*, 2017–, *How Choreography Works*, 2015, *DUELLE* 2009/2021.[1]

You might notice that the dancers move in ways that are not, at first glance, especially virtuosic. The movements may even look quotidian, perhaps like movements we perform every day without noticing what we're doing, and certainly not deliberately incarnated and staged like this. So: everyday gestures deracinated, concentrated, given intention? Perhaps, but not entirely; if so, the intention transforms them radically. Gestures you think you might make, or be able to make, are now made impossible for you—too careful, too technical and prodigious to be only everyday. Too ordinary to be noticed, too noticed to be ordinary, then: a question of what it might mean to be *among*.

These gestures—impressive for their enigmatic deliberativeness, being too fast, too slow, too rhythmic and arrhythmic, too inappropriate, too articulate for the ordinary that they nonetheless encompass—also induce a questioning as to their general sense. The movements are not dance enough to be dance, but also *too much* dance to be dance: dance emerging between the not-enough and the too-much. This opens another question: not just what it means to be *among*, but also *against*. What is dance when it is at once not-enough and too-much to be dance? Dance against itself?

Lasica's dancing poses philosophical or, more directly, *environmental* questions about its own actuality: what is dance such that *this* is dance? And because this question is not only reflexive but conditional, every dance becomes a kind of experiment with minimal and essential conditions of bodies and spaces, engaging expectations about narrative and genre, but also with conceptual criteria of what dance requires to be dance. Among and against, uncoordinated yet compossible, coordinated yet incompossible: a question of *contact*.

What does Lasica's dance think—and not only with feet, but with eyes, hands, foreheads, spaces, costume, sound, all sorts of ambient forces? What does it do that dance today—and *only* dance—can present to us? In the very obscurity of what dance is today? Is it to put bodies and spaces not simply into new contexts, but also into new contacts? Material contacts, for example, in which bodies encounter or even fail to encounter each other in surprising ways, stripped of the usual expectations of aim and interest? But also more abstract contacts too—movements and genre, say, or stories and persons, spaces and institutions?

The aftermath of modernism is one of the determining conceptual and historical contexts for Lasica's project. Modernism—that astonishing efflorescence across the arts that emerged worldwide towards the end of the nineteenth century—testifies to a kind of becoming-planetary of the arts, to the sense of a new connectivity between previously separated geographies and cultures, between heterogenous ways of doing and evaluating. One major feature of modernism is how crucial 'dance' was to it. You perhaps need think only of such famous innovators as Isadora Duncan, Maud Allan, Sophie Taeuber-Arp, Loïe Fuller, Josephine Baker, Martha Graham, Mary Wigman and Vaslav Nijinsky to get a sense of this. What happens in St Petersburg, Vienna, Buenos Aires,

1—*How Choreography Works* and *DUELLE* were co-created with Deanne Butterworth and Jo Lloyd and with Deanne Butterworth respectively.

Mexico City, Tokyo, and so on, now starts to be registered and taken up in other places with an unprecedented rapidity and enthusiasm.

Certainly, this is partially an effect of colonialism, of the enforced submission of peoples by imperial violence and capitalist expansion. In a world of empires, expropriation and appropriation are the watchwords of governance. Anthropological research records and disseminates information about the dance practices of peoples across the world; disciplines as different as philology, archaeology and aesthetics start to recognise dance as a universal art form. Tribal groups perform their 'traditional dances' around the world to paying audiences, on tours initiated by invading settlers and sponsored by entertainment entrepreneurs: in an Australian context, you might think of the commercial Grand Corroboree that took place at the Adelaide Oval in 1885. The European ballet, Noh drama, the Māori haka, ancient Greek choral practices, and so on, start to be connected practically, scientifically and aesthetically—studied, restaged and disseminated across the world in a series of not-altogether-traditional forms.

The emergent communications media, from the telegraph to the gramophone, the typewriter and the radio, also play an important part. Most decisively for dance *per se*, it is the first time in history that some elements of dance—the dancers, costumes, scenes, movements—can be captured and represented by photography, then chronophotography, then cinema itself (whose very name derives from the Greek word for motion). Things that were previously

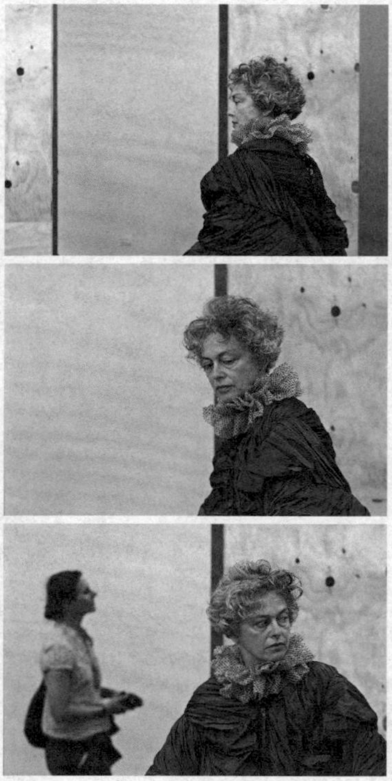

Shelley Lasica, *The Shape of Things to Come* 2016–17, Artspace, Sydney, 9 February – 17 April 2017. Photos: Jessica Maurer

uniquely local now become visible across the planet in new ways and to new eyes with new interests.

This situation reposes old questions with a new intensity, and starts to offer not only new answers, but new kinds of answers. What is dance? Who gets to dance? When? With whom? What movements are permitted and which impermissible, possible and impossible? Why or why not? After all, even in the most supposedly libertarian cultures, you can't just dance anywhere, in any way, at any time. Just try attempting an unscripted animation at your arts board meeting. All cultures tend to order and govern bodies according to extremely clear and strict regulations, and libertarian cultures are never as libertarian as they might seem. On the contrary: dance's links to sacrality, licence and festival raise the most intense and direct anxieties about the proper use and place of bodies. You don't put a male dancer in a tutu; you don't move your arms in traditional Irish dancing; you don't let young people dance unchaperoned or unsurveilled. I shan't go on.

Dance is something that must be identified, named, controlled, limited, excluded, included whenever and wherever it appears. The ancient spectre of the *Tanzverbot*—a ban on dancing—turns out to be immanent to dance itself. Dance bears integrally upon the personal and the political, the sexual and the religious. It does so 'externally', in being an object for customary and legal scrutiny, as well as 'internally', in that types and tokens, genres and gestures, of dance are also formed out of this tension between the ban and its transgression. What is dance, such that everybody can dance and not everybody can dance?

When the limited and inherited aspects of such restrictions become patent—as they did for the modernists—'dance' suddenly takes on a primal, equalising, disequilibrating, universal, material and abstract force. A liberated dance will liberate the body from the chains of its inheritances and institutions. Loïe Fuller, who was, significantly, friends with the great scientists and Nobel Prize-winners Marie and Pierre Curie, explicitly wanted to 'confuse and unite the genres', whirling abstractly in her famous *grande robe* under experimental lighting rigs. Dada's Sophie Taeuber-Arp engaged in radical mixed-media productions at Cabaret Voltaire. Vaslav Nijinsky famously danced in such a way that he exceeded the proper purview and limits of a ballet master.

Such dance breaks with classical European dance, perhaps with all traditional constructions of dance, in attacking theatricality—in terms of the established routines of staging, costuming, setting, narratives, accompaniment, audiences—and accordingly pushes the human body beyond its supposed limits. Through the new dance, Fuller is no longer even 'a woman'; Nijinsky is no longer 'a person'; the Belgian dancer Akarova is no longer even human, having become 'music architecture' and 'living geometry'.[2] The attack on theatricality is also an attack on the customs and orthodoxies of the social world, as it is also an attack on the natural world. Beyond culture and nature, modernist dance communicates with in-human absolutes.

If dance is no longer subordinated to nature or the natural body, to society and customary behaviours, or to theatre as a name and frame for the staging of

2—See Nell Andrew, *Moving Modernism: The Urge to Abstraction in Painting, Dance, Cinema*, Oxford University Press, Oxford, 2020.

physical movement, it is opened to other abstract forms of possible ordering and nomination. Hence the modernist arrival of the choreographer as an assembler of bodies-in-movement. Dance is not or no longer just a basic anthropological constant or one of the arts among others; rather it names the basis of all physical movement and therefore of all the arts.

There is no art without a living body. If dance is the art of the body, there are no other arts without dance. It is therefore fundamental, non-negotiable, even if there are forms of art that might seem to transcend physicality, going beyond this or that body, straining towards an ideal that is not in the world—'the ghostly paradigm of things' that W.B. Yeats saw as the essence of Plato's vision of nature. Since there is no art without a body, and since bodies, beyond their inheritances, are obviously capable of all kinds of strange, even novel movements, this basic capacity for invention by literally *anybody* renders dance the privileged sign of Art Itself, the most fundamental, universal and necessary of the arts. In dance, the body goes beyond itself, its social and natural being, by being only itself.

Shelley Lasica, *The Design Plot* 2017–, 215 Albion Street, Brunswick, Melbourne, 12 July 2018.
Pictured: Louella May Hogan and Lilian Steiner (left); Louella May Hogan and Shelley Lasica (right).
Photos: Jacqui Shelton

The body is active, a movement in space–time. Dance in fact makes space, or remakes spaces (and times), insofar as the purpose of such spaces is no longer set by the exigencies of need and want, as places of survival, of eating and breeding. Dance overcomes, as the German philosopher Friedrich Nietzsche put it, the spirit of gravity: it is never entirely weighty or serious, locked to the earth by immutable force, which is also why it indicates the essence and end of the virtuosic, and why even writing should become 'a dance of the pen'. But the space itself has determinations that can be either affirmed or suppressed as part of the singularity of the dance itself: dance is always in a polemic tension with 'the conditions of space and time'.

This body moves in space–time such that the former is just itself in its active becoming-other-to-itself and the latter is no longer just itself—although

the two can no longer be separated. In a dance, the appearance of the body cannot be divorced from its actuality and activity. It is the liberation of physical appearing as the thing itself. This is again why dance is an image of life: it is nothing but life itself as life overgoing itself as itself, time made according to the dance and not according to need. It can thus take place anywhere, in the street or on the page.

Body–Space–Itself: this trio, supposedly revealed by the artistic-image-of-dance-as-art, confronts the routines and rhetoric of the institutions that are nonetheless committed to transmitting it. The modernists in general despised—or at the very least *professed* to despise—the major institutions of bourgeois modernity. The theatre was a depository of dead gestures and genres, the museum was a mausoleum, the library a festering rat's nest of rotting signs, the schools and the universities mortified children into machines, and so forth. One of the reasons that dance became so important for modernism is because it *escaped* such institutions in fundamental ways: we know, for instance, how difficult it is to represent and transmit dance, even in the most developed forms of choreography as the writing–directing of figures and steps, even in the virtual realities of the present. As the art of the *living* body, dance essentially resists museums, libraries, schools, whatever, all those decaying cemeteries that depended on the semblances of word and wire, wood and image.

For much the same reasons, the modernists make dance at once one kind of art and a name for the essence of art that bears simultaneously on the ethics of non-artistic practices. What does this mean? It means that 'dance' names the obscure but absolute limit at which physical movement—lying, sitting, walking, running, jumping, breathing, and so on—becomes something other than just necessary, just tied to physics and biology. Anyone *can* do it; everyone *is* doing it. Yet not everyone does it the same way, or as well—and this is also part of the point. As a kind of art, dance is fundamental and universal insofar as it forces a reflexive activation of the most basic aspects of animate life itself: one's own movement with others in space becomes a question about the sense and purpose of animation itself, its potentials, its impotencies, its value and evaluation at a cosmic scale. As the French poet Stéphane Mallarmé famously wrote: 'the Dance alone [is] capable, in its summary writing, of translating the fleeting and sudden all the way to the Idea.'

If dance today retains some of these ambitions, it is also the case that the strenuous modernist distinction between art (as life) and institution (as death) is no longer sustainable. On the contrary, dance can no longer be conceptually or practically separated from its own institutions—indeed, 'dance' itself can now appear to be nothing more elevated than a particular, finite kind of anthropologically delimited 'institution'—and these institutions in any case tend now to be more concerned with the contemporary than preserving the past. We might even say that the institutions of the museum, the library, the school, and so on, in fact took on the modernist critique of their backward-looking practices and in so doing turned towards the life of the living they would once have rejected; this turn, moreover, led to a certain absorption of what were once externalities into those institutions themselves. Also, the ever-accelerating intensification of the power of media technologies to simulate with accuracy,

but to create, hybridise and mutate as well, means that some of the key aspects of dance that had evaded inscription and reproduction are now as available for such as any other practice. 'Life' and 'death', the 'active' and the 'passive', find themselves intercalated, complicated, and the differences between presentation and representation cannot be easily decided.

As such, dance can no longer function as an anti-institutional power par excellence; it cannot set itself simply against institutions such as the museum; in fact, dance now seeks to re-emerge *within* them, but on the other side of them. But this has the consequence of rendering indistinct, indiscernible, any specificity to dance, at the very moment that it revivifies the question of dance's tension with(in) itself.

Where does this leave dance today? What is dance today? Is there dance today?

This is where Lasica's work takes up the challenge.

It takes on, in principle, any movement of the body as a possible operation for dance. It takes on the problems posed by genres and institutions, of media and exhibition. It takes on the obscurity of definition of contemporary dance as one of its resources. And it assumes the consequences of these problems as the occasion for experiments in particular spaces with particular bodies at particular times with particular audiences.

It poses questions of the body, according to number and repetition, self and other. Think of the titles of such works as *DUELLE*; *TRIPLEX*, 1993; *Solos for Other People*, 2015. The 'body' itself is involved in a *pas de deux* which is also a *main à main* and a *corps à corps*, a doubling, a halving, a struggle, a becoming-the-other. The body is no longer given as such, but becomes a kind of *objectile*, the objecting projecting of a non-subjective complex of motion. A somatic logic of individuation and de-individuation is at play, between the negation of what a body can do and its apparition in another body, another place. Think too of the sequence in *BEHAVIOUR Part 1*, 1993, in which we find, as Brenda Ludeman says, 'her emotional negotiation of space', and in which, as Judith Pascal puts it, 'the orchestration of the body's movements in terms of repetition and variation emphasises the geometry of its structure'.[3]

It poses questions of spaces according to their names and limits, their expectations of genre and institution: *ACTION SITUATION*, 1999; *LIVE OPERA SITUATION*, 1998; *Play in a Room*, 2003–07. Here there is no single logic to Lasica's 'dance' overall, but efforts tied to the logic of specific spaces and their archaeology of constructions, exploring their size, location and disposition, as well as their institutional impositions and overtones. In *Play in a Room*, witness the isotonic pop and hop, the foot on tiptoe, the twist and the spasm, the unexpected eruption of odd coordinations. Are these causes, correlations, or mere accidents of appearance? The bunching and dispersal of bodies and their parts alludes to classical dance, theatricality, archiving, liveness, the everyday, in their abnormal gesturing.

3—See the contemporaneous catalogue texts for *BEHAVIOUR*, including Brenda Ludeman, 'Shelley Lasica—Accretion', and Judith Pascal, 'Shelley Lasica', in *Shelley Lasica: Behaviour*, exh. cat., Printed Books, Melbourne, 1994, n.p.

It poses questions of movement-as-life in the terms of the expressibility of events: *Happening Simultaneously*, 1991; *Now*, 1989–90; *Something Happens*, 2010; *As We Make It*, 2013–14. This involves the problem of time: of repetitions, digressions, revisions, retroactions and anticipations, aggregating and segregating. There are interrupted developments and information transmitted in the absence of any direct conveyancing.

If the posing of questions about dance in dance can't be answered in any straightforward way, the continuation of the questioning is itself a labour of love, that is, a dance of thinking. The notorious French psychoanalyst Jacques Lacan once offended the MIT linguist Noam Chomsky by asserting 'We think we think with our brains; personally, I think with my feet. That's the only way I really come into contact with anything solid.'[4]

This is what I think has become of modernism in Lasica's work. For the primacy of the living body, we now have the dialectic of *too ordinary to be noticed, too noticed to be ordinary*: the *among*. For the vital activity of that body, we now have the dialectic of *too much to be dance, too little to be dance*: the *against*. And for the emergence of the essence of dance as itself, we now have a paradoxical articulation of the inarticulate: the question of *contact*. What Lasica's dance shows, among other things, is that contemporary dance is simultaneously *among* and *against* itself and its avatars. It is an ongoing sequence of choreographic experiences of *contact*.

That (not) everybody can (not) (want) (to) dance—*is* dance.

Shelley Lasica, *LIVE OPERA SITUATION* 1998, Wesleyan Hall, Albert Park, Melbourne, 15–18, 21–25 July 1998. Video stills: Dance Works (courtesy of Shelley Lasica)

4—Cited in Elizabeth Roudinesco, *Jacques Lacan: Outline of a Life, History of a System of Thought*, Columbia University Press, New York, 1997, p. 378.

Choreographing the Archive: Shelley Lasica's *WHEN I AM NOT THERE*

Zoe Theodore

The first time I met Shelley Lasica—six years ago now—we spoke about how to approach her archive. Almost thirty years into her practice it was as though the accumulation suddenly needed attention. Almost in the same breath, she began to articulate the 'more to do' (Shelley's words, not mine).

So 'let us not begin at the beginning, nor even at the archive'.[1]

* * *

Shelley Lasica's work *WHEN I AM NOT THERE*, 2022, is a disciplinary, analytical response to the conundrum of how to exhibit dance. At the same time it is also a critical confrontation with the prevailing preconceptions of what dance is and what it might do. It is the surveying of one's practice through the collision of choreography as exhibition making and choreography as archiving. It is *choreographing problems* (to borrow Bojana Cvejić's turn of phrase).[2]

As an artist, Shelley is propelled by what her work is not. Not necessarily anti anything, more sceptical of everything. An invitation from Monash University Museum of Art (MUMA) to create an exhibition that returns to her oeuvre, the first of its kind for an Australian choreographer, provided an opportunity for speculative experimentation. Her innate response was to recoil from conservative precedents of the choreographer's retrospective exhibition or archival re-enactment. And this doesn't mean that *WHEN I AM NOT THERE* was developed without considering this historical context, as this specificity intimately informed the work. Because 'context is everything' (Shelley's words again).

Scepticism and methodological reflexivity are alive in Shelley's attempt to choreograph the problem at hand—namely how to exhibit dance and reproaching the preconceptions of what dance is and what it might do. They have engendered a radical approach to a survey exhibition and birthed a choreographic work that charts new territory for practice.

Having made *WHEN I AM NOT THERE* alongside Shelley over the last three years as creative producer, I offer here a compendium of terms as an adjunct to the work.

Critique Methodology

Critique as a methodology is the framework that informs Shelley's process for creating a new work. Understanding this makes one privy to Shelley's modus operandi—to compulsively address context.

Taking a structurally experimental approach, *WHEN I AM NOT THERE* sets its eyes on the practical and logistical parameters of creating a durational

1—Jacques Derrida and Eric Prenowitz, 'Archive Fever: A Freudian Impression', *Diacritics*, vol. 25, no. 2, Johns Hopkins University Press, Baltimore, 1995, p. 9.
2—See Bojana Cvejić, *Choreographing Problems: Expressive Concepts in European Contemporary Dance and Performance*, Palgrave Macmillan, London, 2015.

performance for a museum and confounds them with conceptual approaches to performance and display. It is a complex and yet surprisingly nimble intertextual framework that allows for moments of return.

Shelley's work doesn't use instructional scores. Her oeuvre isn't a continuation of the Cagean preoccupation with seriality or mathematical organisational systems. Nor does she set large amounts of choreographic sequencing and direct it to be performed in unison. So how then does she create a durational work that can at once look back and propel itself into the future?

Shelley Lasica, *The Design Plot* 2017–, Bus Projects, Melbourne, 30 November 2019. Pictured (left): Ellen Davies and Lilian Steiner. Photos: Jacqui Shelton

This is approached by looking for patterns and possible connections, as if solving a puzzle. Problems of space and the organisation of time were fundamental considerations in this equation. So too was deliberation on the objects that share the space with the dance (costumes, props, sound) and their potential existence beyond the choreographic mechanism. Questions of being in or being out are answered with 'everything must exist within this world'. Like a shape within a shape, they are to be perceived in the context of the performance. Not parataxis, but syntaxis.

Inclusive of new sequences born of physical research and historical choreographies (each of which Shelley dubs 'episodes'), *WHEN I AM NOT THERE* occupies the architecture of the gallery and the temporality of an exhibition by leaving form in flux and open to in situ reconfiguration. Budgetary constraints and physical capacity influenced performance hours, and in turn became additional parameters for the methodology. Gallery architecture and the division of sightlines means the impossibility of viewing the dance from a singular perspective is thrown in the mix. The historical relationship between solo and ensemble work goes into the pot, along with the question of the relationship between different choreographic modes (known and improvised). This pot logic is methodological and not referential. 'The methodology is cognisant of the situation we are in,' says Shelley, 'but it's not descriptive.' By

this, she means that specificity is the logic of the task at hand, but don't be mistaken, this is not the material.

Systems of Knowledge

Shelley practises a way of working that isn't dogmatic. This method supports the creation of a mechanism that has its own motor that continues to run whether the audience is tending to it or not. It is a vehicle that supports the creation of something else.

Rehearsal images, Shelley Lasica, *WHEN I AM NOT THERE* 2022, Princes Park, Melbourne, 27 October 2021. Photos: Jacqui Shelton

A true studio artist, Shelley sets up working conditions with a specific group of dancers in which they interrogate physical research and then manifest it into a physical language. The practice of physical research enables this group to discover its unknown potential through an iterative process of undertaking and refining collective somatic exploration to create systems of knowledge and choreographic material. This cooperative of minds and bodies stays with the work into perpetuity, as recasting has never been considered a possibility by Shelley. It is precisely the transference of these systems of knowledge that is the method.

Using choreography as a tool for analysis and production, choreography enables Shelley to store corporeal memory within an intersubjective group of living organisms. She examines the consumption of information and the act of transference before this research is disseminated via the collective body.

Rehearsal image, Shelley Lasica, *WHEN I AM NOT THERE* 2022, Drawing Studio, Monash Art, Design and Architecture, Melbourne, 31 January – 4 February 2022. Pictured: Lana Šprajcer and Megan Payne. Photo: Jacqui Shelton

Physical Language

Shelley is fond of elliptical remarks and elliptical movements. Her virtuosity is so apparent you'd be a fool to miss it. The dancers jump from the sublime to the ludicrous so deftly—as quickly as you might notice a dancer's tiny shift in attention or a shift in weight. The challenge is not to overdo it and to notice the vulnerability that can result. For me, the seemingly anti-virtuosic movements are a red herring for somatic acuity.

When I think of the dancing, there is a certain je ne sais quoi of Shelley's physical language. Movements appear irrational but not incidental. Mysterious but not abstract. Elusive but not illegible. They give pause to wonder at how to quantify the effort to make a gesture look effortless.

Choreography arranges information through time and space via bodies. But don't be mistaken, Shelley isn't just arranging or making shapes vis-á-vis the performing bodies and prosaic gestures. And yet, you might notice a dancer describing a shape to you via movement soaked in that Shelley-like postured listlessness, a kind of invested detachment.

Rehearsal images, Shelley Lasica, *WHEN I AM NOT THERE* 2022, Drawing Studio, Monash Art, Design and Architecture, Melbourne, 31 January – 4 February 2022. Pictured (top): LJ Connolly-Hiatt, Lana Šprajcer, Luke Fryer, Shelley Lasica and Timothy Harvey. Photos: Jacqui Shelton

Agency

Conversations during the pandemic became the initial forum for creating the work, with each performer or consultant a building-block imperative to its foundations. A gathering of individuals, *WHEN I AM NOT THERE* is a case of collective creation—a concept that challenges the traditional authorship in the visual arts, a discipline that is still unpicking the historical notion of a singular artist 'genius'.

Dynamic Linkage

Shelley's tone of ethereal remarks and ellipsical movement, the symphony is so apparent as not to be a focus in it. The dancer's limbs from the subtitle to the imborous so lightly – so quickly – you no longer notice audiences only, still in a moment of sculptural weight. The challenges open to us all: learn to notice the vulnerability that can easily arise in the scene itself, anti-virtuosity is evident in every rendering, for somatic accord.

When I think of the dancing either way, certain is the safe craft of Shelley, one of Hopkins, Meerman – appearances that not for in identity, even cases but not substantial have an isn't figured. They are prone to wonder at how to gentry, the effort to make it sensuous in its efforts.

Choreography to stage a fleeting infomration encounter, not a spectator bodies. Be doing, or implicit in Shelley, very performance or making shapes vis-à-vis the performing nodes and passive gestures. And see, you might notice in dances designing a shape to you in movements, sealed in that Shelley, thee painful audiences, a trained investigated achievement.

Editorial Issues: Shelley Lasica in *Why Is There Something Instead of Nothing?* Abu Dhabi and Saathi-Gaard, Gallery, NSW Sydney, 2014. Photo: Paul Arora. Commission Presentation Society, Louvre Capital City Tower at Art Industry Towers. Photo: Dominik Mercier.

In general,

Conversations during the symposium became the vehicle for that for keeping the world. With each performance concerning a particular piece, it imperative that I found things. A releasing of individuality. Where I AM WITH THOUGHT – sure of coherence, somehow – a concern that perhaps one traditional authorship is the structural as a valuable thank still implicating the historical horizons a singular dancer pointed.

Preferencing shared experiences means creation depends on the determination of individuals and how information is transferred intersubjectively. A complex game of exquisite corpse, key pieces of the puzzle at times lie with a singular performer. Like a script with portions of a protagonist's responsive dialogue missing, elements of *WHEN I AM NOT THERE* exist only within an individual's somatic experience during the development of the work.

The passing of information from dancer to dancer is not the information's death but a moment for transference, absorption and individual agency. This manner of working relies on the systems of knowledge being embodied by the specific group of dancers, who are given agency during the work's development and its performance. They can each trigger change within the methodological mechanism, so configurations slip and slide as they stitch together the work's episodes—with each day comes a new renegotiation or the latest chapter in a chronicle of problem-solving.

Context

What does it mean to dance in a museum? What is the raison d'être and what are the potential aesthetic stakes?

Having performed in galleries for nearly the entirety of her career, this context became a breeding ground for early experimentation for Shelley, one free from binding historical references or discipline docility. Now, thirty years later, this form has built its own narrative and trajectory, and speaks to the lineages of both performance art history and conceptual dance.

In the art museum we have a ready frame of reference to performance art history, but what is 'conceptual dance'? Seth Price has described conceptual practice as 'privileging framing and context, and constantly renegotiating its relationship to its audience'.[3] Bojana Cvejić describes the paradigm shift in European contemporary dance of the 1990s as the 'theoretical and political questioning of dance's medium historicity, institutional regulation and spectatorship, comparable to post-conceptual art'.[4]

So, what can the museum give to conceptual dance beyond space and funding? *WHEN I AM NOT THERE* critically examines its offerings, namely: new modes of spectatorship divorced from the static attention commanded by going to a theatre; the emancipation from a singular performance axis (a defining feature of a dance that isn't performed on a proscenium arch stage); and a durational temporality defined by opening hours.

Theatrical Devices

Modulation is driven by theatrical devices rather than narrative. There are no attempts to convey a narrative, an arch or crescendo, but that isn't to say that narrative isn't used as a device in *WHEN I AM NOT THERE*. Littered by

3—Seth Price, 'Dispersion', in David Maroto, Joanna Zielińska (eds), *Artist Novels: The Book Lovers Publication*, Sternberg Press, Berlin, 2015, p. 111.
4—Bojana Cvejić, 'European Contemporary Dance, before its Recent Arrival in the Museum', in Cosmin Costinaş and Ana Janevski (eds), *Is the Living Body the Last Thing Left Alive? The New Performance Turn, Its Histories and Its Institutions*, Para Site, Hong Kong / Sternberg Press, Berlin, 2018, p. 30.

paradoxical speech, the dance carries out like collusive behaviour, with the act of speaking employed without abdicating the meaning of the work.

Phrases of stillness or moments in between act as palate cleansers, undaunted by containment. Not merely transitions but complete acts in themselves that underscore more avenues for interpretation. This stillness foreshadows the affective power of the kinetic articulations that follow, with the images created by the dancer's body caught in a stillness that terminates representation for affect.

Rehearsal images, Shelley Lasica, *BEHAVIOUR Part 7* 2018, Carlton Baths Stadium, Melbourne, 1 February 2018. Photos: Jacqui Shelton

And let's talk about gaze. These dancers look at you and at each other, rejecting the archetypal contemporary dancer's gaze, where the performer seems to be looking somewhere beyond you. This directive of active looking, coupled with an apparently scalding assessment of performance's existence and insistence on being watched, I identify as the desire for and spirit of transgression. The disembodied spectatorial gaze customary to the theatre is remodelled via the proximity and presence of the performers and the palpable experience of transference this creates. In an act of radical reflexivity, the gaze allows the performances to reconfigure the habitation of space by both audience and performer.

Shelley Lasica, *Solos for Other People* 2015, Carlton Baths Stadium, Melbourne, 13–22 March 2015. Pictured: Lee Serle. Photo: Gregory Lorenzutti

Doing

The *doing* is what concerns Shelley. Uninterested in replication or mimesis, nor the mere representation of the work, Shelley is instead preoccupied with 'posing the problems associated with the making, performance, and attending of performance'.[5] *WHEN I AM NOT THERE* highlights the difference in affect between movement performed and movement perceived by the viewer. It is not that one is more authentic or correct than the other, but that they don't necessarily correspond—and that's okay.

The impulse to give the work an afterlife doesn't come into play for Shelley, who is more interested in the true a-liveness of the work. Her rejection of a drilled-down, objectified, singular, autonomous artwork is accentuated by her commitment to sticking with the tension inherent in the instability of dance. She is not trying to emulate the material but to think through it corporeally. Within the performative moment, Shelley and her dancers are *doing* embodied decision-making—they are *doing* the description of a shape, not just creating an image of it.

In a conversation with Rhiannon Newton about her work *Doing Dancing,* Erin Brannigan describes Shelley's prowess as a 'commitment to the multiplicities of the decentered corporeal field, suspending the shift away from experience and towards a focused form of cognition'.[6] This account also reminds me of Bojana Cvejić's description of this kind of dancing as a practice that could 'be explained by a turn away from the ideological mechanisms of interpellation and representation and towards affective experiential embodiment'.[7]

Semiotic Probing

To figure / The figure
To shape / The shape
To exhibit / The exhibit
To display / The display
To perform / The performance

In an attempt to make sense of something somatically (it's the conundrum again) Shelley would often ask the dancers to think about the problem via language, without falling into the trap of chasing utopian or ideological ideas. For example: Is it exposition or disposition?

In a discussion regarding the interrogation of 'figuring' in its verbal sense, Shelley remarked that *WHEN I AM NOT THERE* consultant Lisa Radford linked it with the phrase 'figure and ground' from art history. Informed by Gestalt psychology, the concept of figure-ground perception describes the way in which the mind perceives images and distinguishes an object or figure from its background. Reflecting on this conversation, I began

5 — Cvejić, 'European Contemporary Dance, before its Recent Arrival in the Museum', p. 32.
6 — Erin Brannigan and Rhiannon Newton, 'Propositions for Doing Dancing', *Runway*, no. 36, 2018, accessed 30 Jan 2021, http://runway.org.au/propositions-dancing/.
7 — Cvejić, 'European Contemporary Dance, before its Recent Arrival in the Museum', p. 31.

to think about the notion of the Gestalt, that the whole of anything is greater than its individual parts. And because the embodied perception required by performance is different to what we need in perceiving two-dimensional images, if we expand perception to other modalities including temporal information processing, hearing and listening, and kinaesthetic empathy, what constitutes the whole of *WHEN I AM NOT THERE*? Our perception of the work is further complicated by the presence of both performing and audience subjects, as well as objects in transition via the agency of such subjects. Thus, the whole of the work also encompasses a process of subjectification by the audience subject, where they recognise themselves as a domain for possible knowledge and apprehension.

Returning

During the process of making *WHEN I AM NOT THERE* Shelley said to me numerous times that she is terrified that she is making the same old work new again. Instead, I recognise her suspicion as what I imagine the synchronicity of accumulation, repetition and reflection would feel like. I recognise her suspicion as a returning, or choreography as archiving.

This idea of returning can be contrasted with the perception that performance disappears, or that performance's ontological authenticity can be found in its existence in the manically charged present. Rebecca Schneider points out that this latter attitude, a trend in 1990s performance theory, is well suited to 'the museal context where performance appeared to challenge object status and seemed to refuse the archive its privileged "savable" original'.[8] Performance, and I would argue dance more specifically, is not singular or static but iterative and itinerant. Qualities I also believe an exhibition possesses. So it's not surprising that an exhibition whose material is an archive and method is performative is grappling with objecthood and singularity.

And in this practice of returning Shelley isn't only recalling her own oeuvre; she is also returning to the tropes that have propelled or motivated her in the past. For instance, the ritual of dressing, which she used as a performative trope in *Square Dance BEHAVIOUR Part 6*, 1996–97, and *DRESS*, 1998, appears to reference lineages that go back to Anna Halprin's tour de force *Parades and Changes*, 1965. Another can be identified in the moments of stillness when the dancers observe one another, a trope used by Merce Cunningham in *Squaregame*, which premiered at the Adelaide Festival in 1976—and was attended by a fifteen-year-old Shelley. During that festival, Merce Cunningham also performed a work at the Apollo Stadium, a sports gymnasium, a revelation at the time in terms of the contextual and spatial possibilities for contemporary dance, a propelling impulse evident throughout Shelley's career and a direct reference within *Solos for Other People*, 2015.

While talking about referencing, Shelley and Colby Vexler, a consultant on *WHEN I AM NOT THERE*, questioned whether knowledge or provenance can be acknowledged without having to hold the burden of meaning and intention. They spoke about the referencing tool of a footnote and its potential to be

8 — Rebecca Schneider, *Performing Remains: Art and War in Times of Theatrical Reenactment*, Routledge, London, 2011, p. 98.

adopted as a mode that excuses the work proper from didactic conformity. Footnoting as a concept is explored for its potential to delineate a performance history (or returning), acknowledge past collaborators and support assertions—without performance documentation or wall texts. As I am writing, the question of how to harness the essence of footnotes remains an unresolved puzzle—and we still don't know if a solution will elude us.

Shelley Lasica with Martin Grant, *DRESS* (first performed 1998), Anna Schwartz Gallery, Melbourne, 8–9 November 2019. Photo: Jacqui Shelton

Becoming

The mechanism established for *WHEN I AM NOT THERE* allows for the persistence of Shelley's choreography, propelling itself into continual circulation and evolution through the interrelationship of the performers. Moving beyond André Lepecki's notion of the body as archive, with the dancing body the container for the archive,[9] *WHEN I AM NOT THERE* is a choreographic mechanism for archiving. It is the iterative nature of embodied practice that means that choreography is a mode that is pregnant with potential for arousing collective memory and archiving.

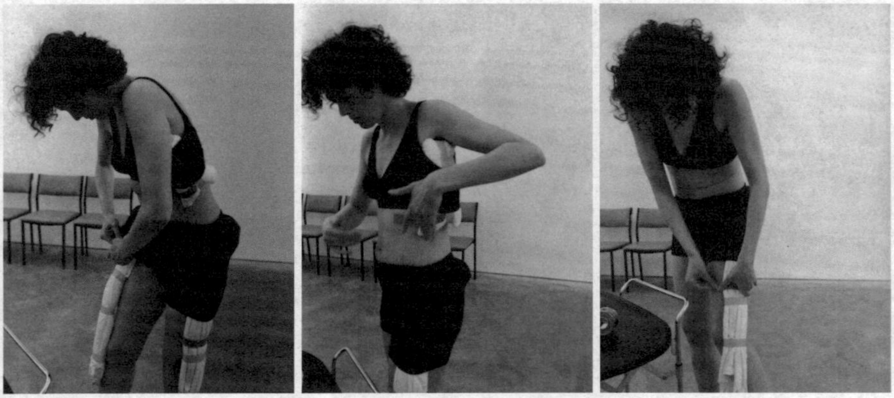

Shelley Lasica, *Square Dance BEHAVIOUR Part 6* 1996–97, Anna Schwartz Gallery, Melbourne, 5–8 December 1996. Photos: Kate Gollings

9— See André Lepecki, 'The Body as Archive: Will to Re-Enact and the Afterlives of Dances', *Dance Research Journal*, vol. 42, no. 2, 2010, pp. 28–48.

What we have is a methodology of keeping a practice alive into perpetuity and information being stored in bodies and transmitted between bodies by repeatedly returning. The collective returning and then becoming in *WHEN I AM NOT THERE* draws me to the Deleuzian concept of becoming. Here the archive and the dancing body function as markers of change, transformation or 'becoming'. Becoming is a determining feature of dance. It reminds me of Henri Bergson's description of reality's temporality as a 'perpetual becoming. It makes itself or it unmakes itself, but it is never something made.'[10] Not only does this speak to the impermanence and the instability of dance, it also speaks to the deterioration of memory vis-á-vis the persistence of objects over time.

One of the episodes in *WHEN I AM NOT THERE* is the dancing of set material that Shelley asked the dancers to learn via video. This prompt was previously used for *VIANNE*, 2008–09, and the material is rehearsal footage that now exists as video documentation. When giving the dancers instruction to learn the material she asked them not to simply learn the movement and sequence but to read and perform the phrase as if they were 'being me'. This prompt speaks to a process that is different from cognition and results in the dancer becoming the container of Shelley's archive, the body archive beyond the signifier.

Crisis of the Object

What is the crisis of the object? It is the tension of production and arrival, or the turmoil between planning and the plan. After a conversation regarding this predicament Colby shared the following quote by architect Junya Ishigami: 'Planning while making the plan's intent no longer visible becomes the intent of this plan.'[11] So what happens if we don't connect the dots? An absence is created—and this is an extremely fertile space for novel creation.

When Shelley talks of the crisis of the object, I relate this to the idea of absence as a means for conceptual production. So, what is Shelley's object? Let's say that the object in *WHEN I AM NOT THERE* is Shelley's entire performance archive, or her body of work and its precariousness in relation to objecthood. For example, while a costume is an object, it is not the absent object in *WHEN I AM NOT THERE*. Instead, the costume represents a trace of something that is left behind—namely the historical performance—which is signified via the trace. What is lacking or absent is the re-staging of historical performances or the presence of them via video documentation as mere representation. Therefore, the signifier is the entire world created by *WHEN I AM NOT THERE*, including objects as traces and episodes from historical choreographies, and the signified is Shelley's answer to the choreographic problem of how to perform one's own archive. And because there are only signifiers in the signifying chain, choreography as archiving is the effect of the signifier and could precede it.[12]

I relate Shelley's 'crisis of objects' to desire, and therefore cannot identify it by any singular thing or person. It doesn't exist in the constructed world of

10— Henri Bergson, *Creative Evolution*, Dover Publications, Mineola, NY, 1998, p. 72.
11— Junya Ishigami, *Another Scale of Architecture*, Seigensha Art Publishing, Kyoto, 2011, p. 187.
12—Jacques Lacan tells us this in *Écrits*, Editions du Seuil, Paris, 1966, p. 468.

WHEN I AM NOT THERE but paradoxically produces effect by setting desire in motion. Or Shelley's desire for the more to do.[13]

* * *

In response to telling people that I write about dance, I regularly get told that dance seems like a private joke or party to which they are not invited. Comprehension and impenetrability are the usual complaints.

Once, when Shelley and I spoke about this inkling, she remarked that this is a false narrative. All of us have a relationship to bodies, movement and sensation, which are the fundamental tools for apprehending dance. Trust yourself (my words).

Rehearsal images, Shelley Lasica, *WHEN I AM NOT THERE* 2022, Drawing Studio, Monash Art, Design and Architecture, Melbourne, 31 January – 4 February 2022. Pictured (left): LJ Connolly-Hiatt, Luke Fryer, Megan Payne and Lana Šprajcer. Photos: Jacqui Shelton

13 — I would like to thank Lou Hourigan, Thomas Baring and Ella Cattach for their generous thoughts in developing these ideas.

Appearing to Create Something Solid
Turning Away the Affect of a Mystery
Now
BELIEVE
DRESS
The Idea of It

Medium	solo performance
Venue	Extensions, Melbourne
Dates	28 July and 4 August 1984
Event	Dance '84, 26 July – 11 August 1984
Costumes	Margaret Lasica
Photography	Rehearsal images by Roger Wood

A

Medium	solo performance
Venue	Athenaeum Theatre 2, Melbourne
Dates	6–9 August 1987
Set and objects	Roger Wood
Costumes	Martin Grant and Fiona Scanlan
Lighting	Nathan Thompson
Photography	Roger Wood (pp. 137–44)
	Andrea Paton (pp. 140–41, 144)
Videography	Simon Burton (pp. 146–49)

B

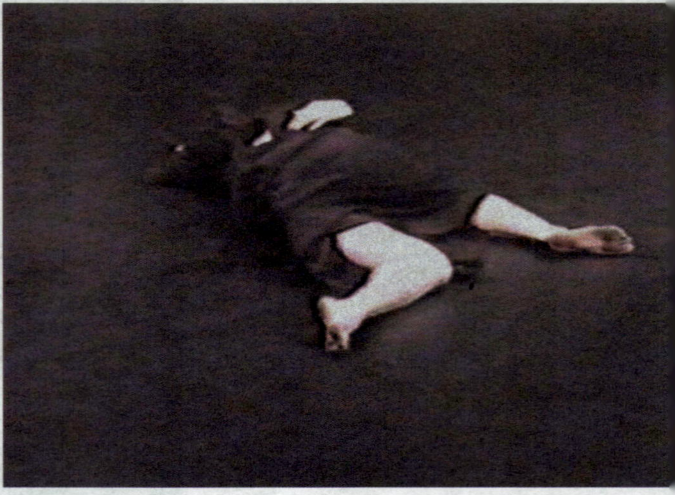

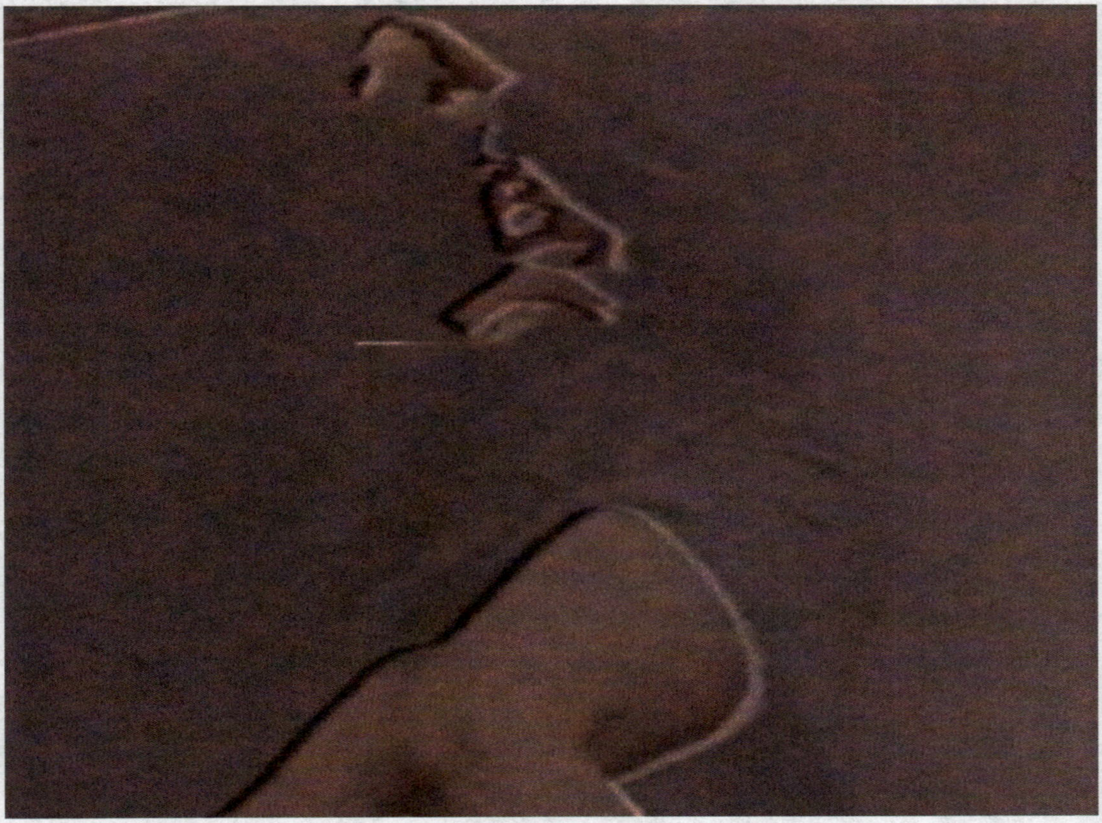

Medium	solo performance
Venue	City Gallery, Melbourne
Dates	30 November – 2 December 1989
Set design	Roger Wood
Paper text artworks	Shiralee Saul
Video	Sylvie Mackie
Costume	Fiona Scanlan
Music	Toshiro Mayuzumi Maurice Ravel Jeff Beck Madonna
Photography	John Betts (pp. 153–55, 158, 161–62, 164–65, 168) Roger Wood (pp. 157, 159, 163, 167)

Medium	solo performance
Venue	City Gallery, Melbourne
Dates	30 November, 1–2 December 1990
Set design	Roger Wood
Scenery	Tony Clark
Photography	Roger Wood

)RESS 181–203 **E1**

Medium	**solo performance**
Venue	**Anna Schwartz Gallery, Melbourne**
Dates	**12–15 February 1998**
Event	**Woolmark Melbourne Fashion Festival**
Costume	**Martin Grant**
Photography	**Kate Gollings (pp. 181–97)**
Videography	**Roger Wood (pp. 198–203)**

)RESS 204–215 **E2**

Medium	**solo performance**
Venue	**Anna Schwartz Gallery, Melbourne**
Dates	**8–9 November 2019**
Event	**Melbourne International Arts Festival**
Costume	**Martin Grant**
Photography	**Jacqui Shelton**

Medium	solo performance
Venue	Anna Schwartz Gallery, Melbourne
Dates	20–22 October 2006
Costumes	Kara Baker and Shelley Lasica for PROJECT
Sound score	Milo Kossowski
Photography	Rohan Young

BEHAVIOUR series
CHARACTER X
Situation series

BEHAVIOUR Part 1 243–251 **G1.1**

Medium	**solo performance**
Venue	**Store 5, Melbourne**
Dates	**24–28 November 1993**
Photography	**Roger Wood**

BEHAVIOUR by Margie Medlin 252–257 **G1.2**

Medium	**video based on the solo performance at Store 5**
Year	**1994**
Duration	**12 minutes**
Sound design	**Dan Witton**

BEHAVIOUR Part 1 and 2 259–265 **G2**

Medium	**solo performance**
Venue	**Athenaeum Theatre, Melbourne**
Dates	**5–7 May 1994**
Photography	**Roger Wood**

Here BEHAVIOUR Part 4 267–275 **G3**

Medium	**solo performance**
Venue	**Anna Schwartz Gallery, Melbourne**
Dates	**11–14 May 1995**
Photography	**Rehearsal images by Kate Gollings**

Square Dance BEHAVIOUR Part 6 277–291 **G4**

Medium	**solo performance**
Venue	**Anna Schwartz Gallery, Melbourne**
Dates	**5–8 December 1996**
Photography	**Kate Gollings**

Medium	ensemble performance
Venue	215 Albion Street, Brunswick, Melbourne
Date	8 September 2018
Event	TO DO / TO MAKE, curated by Shelley Lasica and Zoe Theodore in association with Neon Parc
Performers	Deanne Butterworth Ellen Davies LJ Connolly-Hiatt Luke Fryer Timothy Harvey Alice Heyward Louella May Hogan Benjamin Hurley Rebecca Jensen Leah Landau Shelley Lasica Jo Lloyd Caroline Meaden Daniel Newell Megan Payne Bronwyn Ritchie Harrison Ritchie-Jones Lilian Steiner Jo White
Producer	Zoe Theodore
Photography	Jacqui Shelton

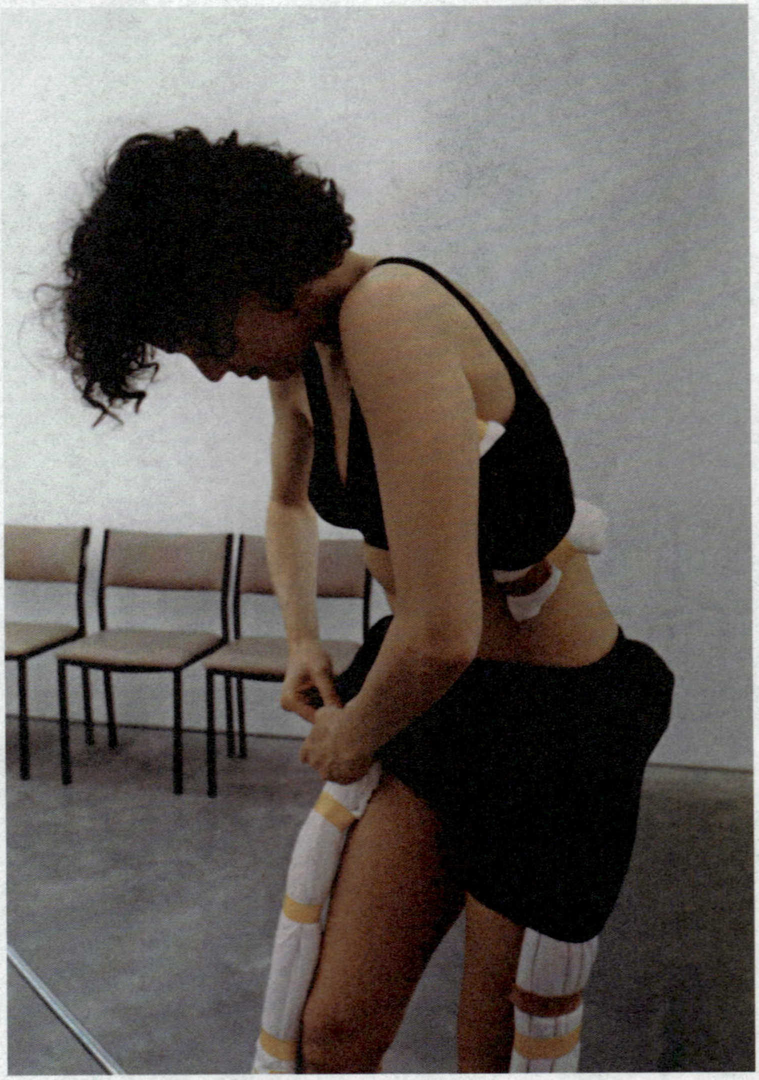

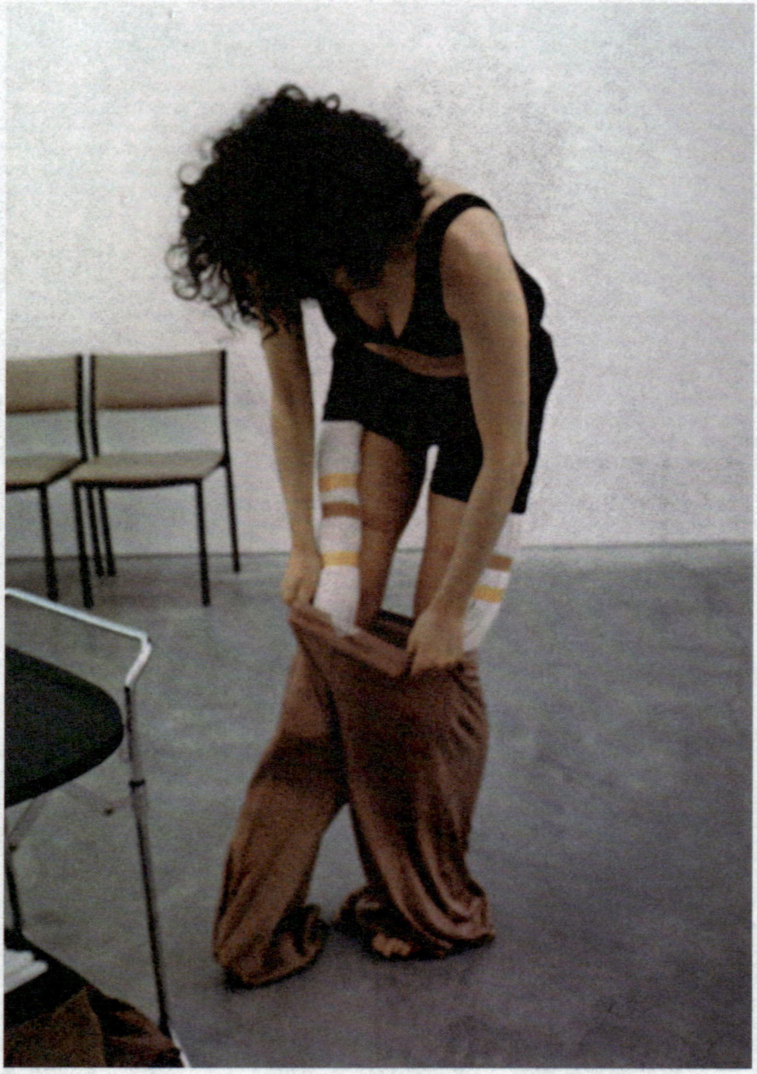

Medium	ensemble performance
Venue	Fitzroy Town Hall, Melbourne
Dates	23 May – 1 June 1996
Event	Next Wave Festival
Performers	Deanne Butterworth Shelley Lasica Carlee Mellow Sandra Parker Kylie Walters
Construction and lighting design	Roger Wood
Costumier and visual design	Kathy Temin
Composer	Paul Schütze
Lighting consultant	Hamish Inglis
Stage manager	Elizabeth Keen
Postcard design	Yanni Florence
Project management	Wendy Lasica
Photography	Kate Gollings (pp. 306–20) Publicity images by Polly Borland (pp. 329–35)
Videography	Roger Wood (pp. 322–25) Robert Falso (pp. 326–27)

1 6 1996

1 6 1996

1 6 1996

1 6 1996

1 6 1996

1 6 1996

1 6 1996

ve drama situation 340–343 I1

Medium	solo performance
Venue	Cleveland, London
Date	27 May 1997
Videography	Deborah Saxon

ITUATION LIVE: THE SUBJECT 345–353 I2

Medium	duet performance
Venue	La Mama, Melbourne
Dates	12–23 November 1997
Performers	Deanne Butterworth Jo Lloyd
Stage manager	Elizabeth Keen
Script	Robyn McKenzie
Costumes	Shelley Lasica (concept) Shio Otani (design)
Music composition	François Tétaz
Photography	Publicity images by Kate Gollings

CTION SITUATION 355–367 I3

Medium	trio performance
Venue	East Wing Gallery, Immigration Museum, Melbourne
Dates	12–14, 18–20 February 1999
Performers	Deanne Butterworth Jo Lloyd Kylie Walters
Script	Robyn McKenzie
Costumes	Kara Baker and Shelley Lasica for PROJECT
Sound score	François Tétaz
Lighting	John Ford
Photography	Publicity images by Kate Gollings (pp. 355–57, 365) Rohan Young (pp. 359–63)

IVE OPERA SITUATION 368–373 **I4**

Medium	ensemble performance
Venue	Wesleyan Hall, Albert Park, Melbourne
Dates	15–18, 21–25 July 1998
Performers	Belinda Cooper Jo Lloyd Carlee Mellow Rachel Roberts
Costumes	Shelley Lasica
Sound score	François Tétaz
Videography	Dance Works (courtesy of Shelley Lasica)

istory Situation 375–389 **I5**

Medium	ensemble performance
Venue	Horti Hall, Melbourne
Dates	14–17, 21–24 March 2002
Event	L'Oréal Melbourne Fashion Festival
Performers	Deanne Butterworth Timothy Harvey Jacob Lehrer Jo Lloyd Bronwyn Ritchie
Video	Ben Speth
Backdrop	Roger Wood
Script	Robyn McKenzie
Costumes	Richard Nylon
Sound score	François Tétaz
Lighting	Roger Wood
Invitation image	Daniel von Sturmer
Photography	Rohan Young

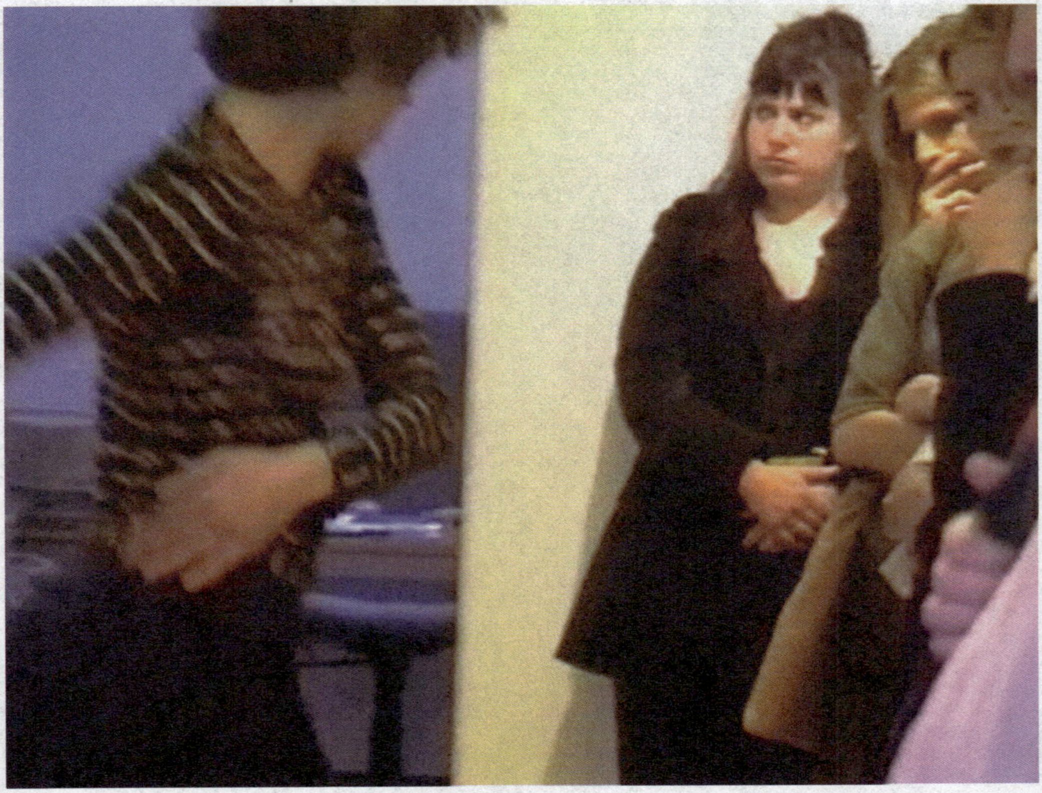

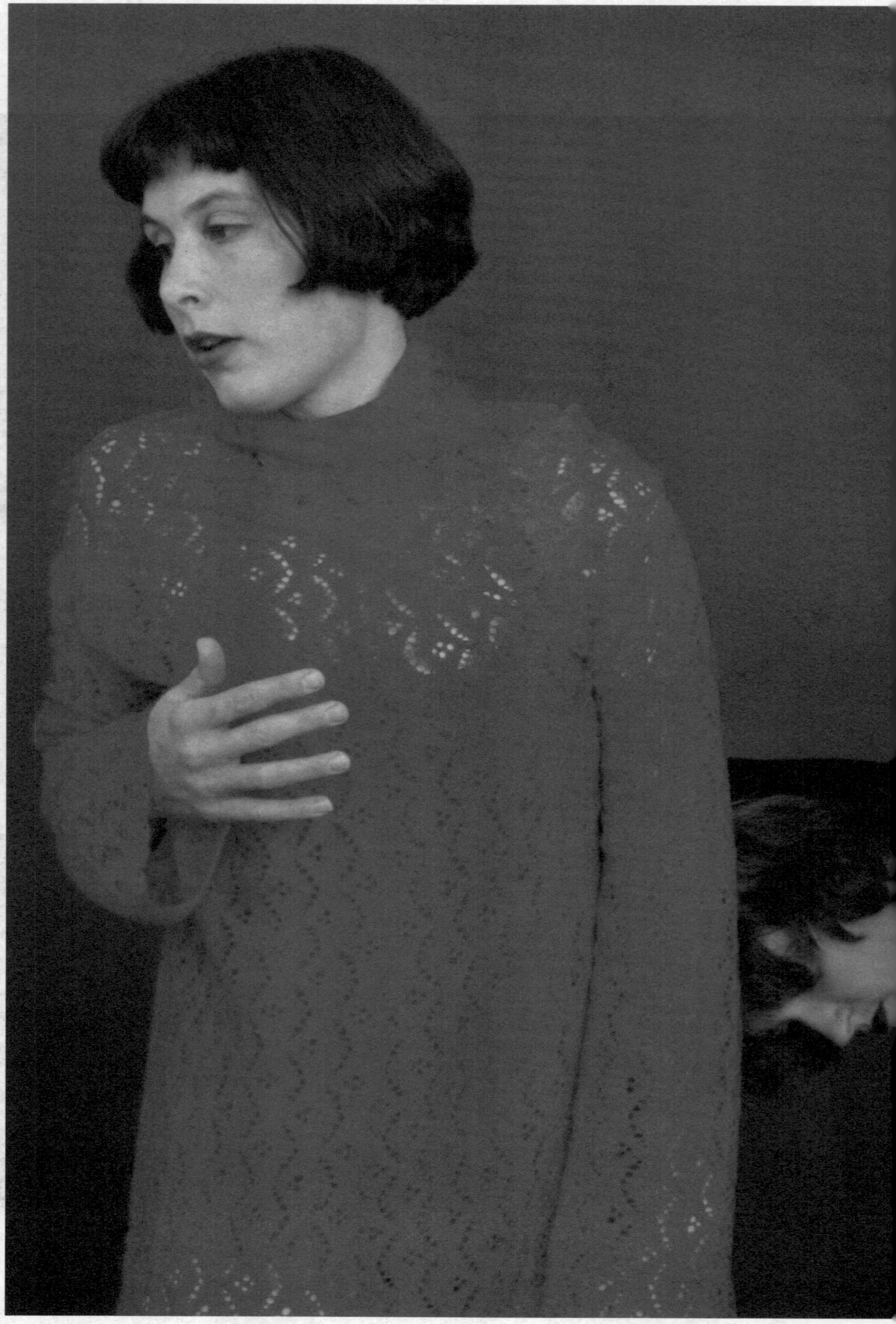

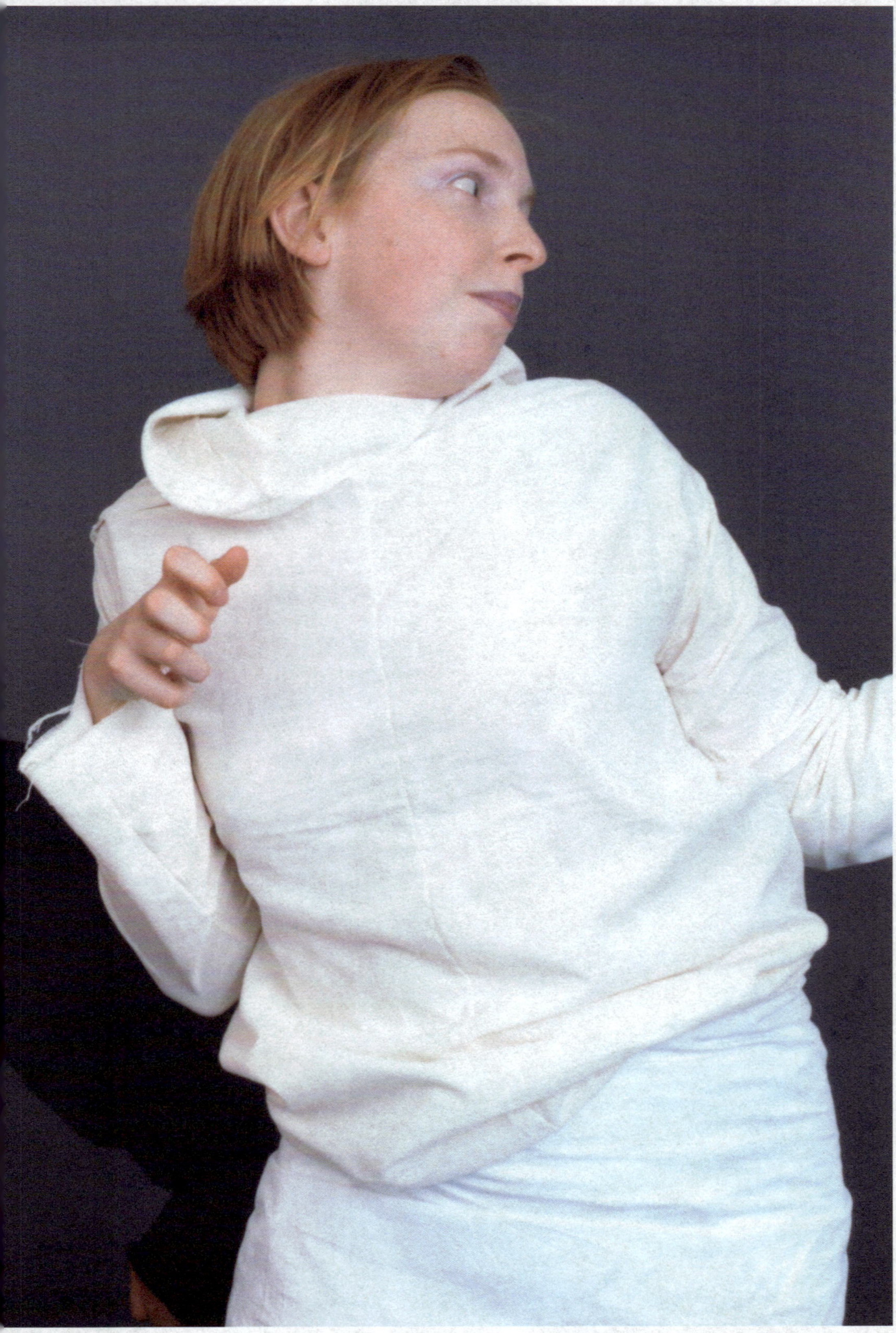

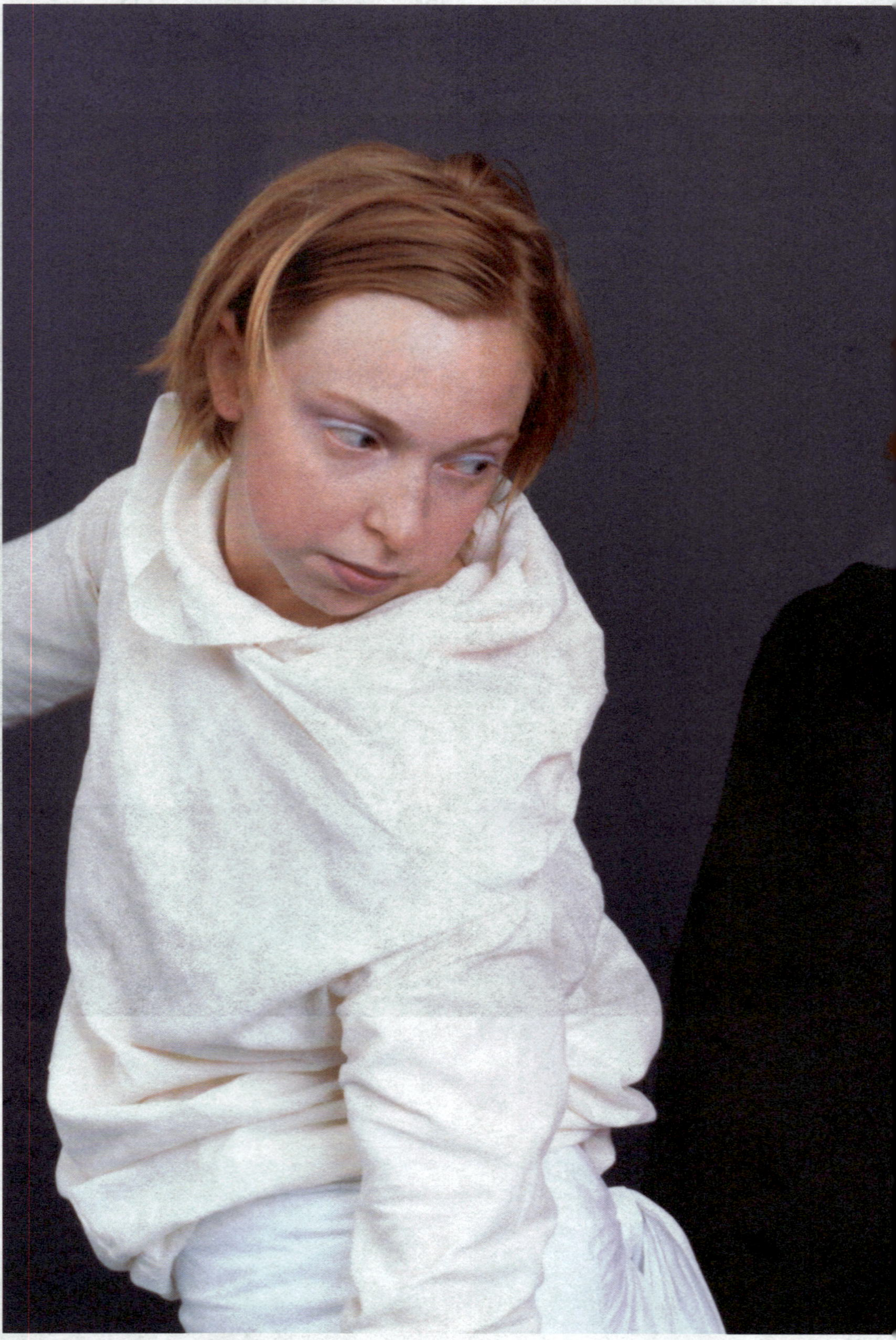

EXIT

EXIT

EXIT

EXIT

VIANNE
VIANNE AGAIN
INSIDE VIANNE AGAIN (National Gallery of Victoria)

VIANNE 396–417 J1

Medium	ensemble performance
Venue	fortyfivedownstairs, Melbourne
Dates	3–14 December 2008
Performers	Deanne Butterworth
	Timothy Harvey
	Jo Lloyd
	Bonnie Paskas
	Lee Serle
Mise-en-scène	Anne-Marie May
Costumes	Kara Baker and Shelley Lasica for PROJECT
Music	Milo Kossowski and Morgan McWaters for PEACE OUT!
Lighting and design consultant	Bluebottle (Ben Cobham)
Invitation design	Milo Kossowski
Text for program notes	Fiona Hile
Curatorium	Ben Speth
	Milo Kossowski
	Robyn McKenzie
	Anne-Marie May
Diffusion	Rachel Young
Project management	Moriarty's Project Inc
Production management	Bluebottle (Bernadette Sweeney and Adam Hardy)
Technical operation	Jenny Hector
Interns	Holly Durant
	Kelly Jirsa
	Madeleine Krenek
	Shian Law
Photography	Rohan Young

VIANNE AGAIN 419–421 J2

Medium	ensemble performance
Venue	RMIT Design Hub, Melbourne
Date	5 September 2013
Performers	Deanne Butterworth
	Timothy Harvey
	Jo Lloyd
	Bonnie Paskas
Mise-en-scène	Anne-Marie May
Wardrobe	Shelley Lasica
Sound score	Milo Kossowski
	Morgan McWaters
Videography	Rohan Young

(National Gallery of Victoria)

by Shelley Lasica, Anne-Marie May and Helen Grogan

Medium	ensemble performance and video installation: 2-channel HD digital video, 4-channel sound; single-channel HD digital video, sound; 12 minutes, looped
Venue	National Gallery of Victoria, Melbourne
Dates	22 November 2013 – 23 March 2014
Event	Melbourne Now
Performers	Deanne Butterworth Timothy Harvey Jo Lloyd Bonnie Paskas
Videographer and camera technician	Anna Gilby
Camera technician	Laura May Grogan
NGV sound design	Benjamin Walbrook
Wardrobe	Shelley Lasica
Photography	Laura May Grogan and Helen Grogan

Solos for Other People
How Choreography Works
How How Choreography Works

Medium	ensemble performance
Venue	Carlton Baths Stadium, Melbourne
Dates	13–22 March 2015
Event	Dance Massive 2015
Performers	Natalie Abbott Deanne Butterworth Timothy Harvey Shelley Lasica Jo Lloyd Daniel Newell Bonnie Paskas Lily Paskas Deborah Saxon Lee Serle Kylie Walters
Producers	Kara Ward Kyle Kremerskothen
Stage manager	Amy Bagshaw
Composition	Anne-Marie May
Costumes	Belinda Hellier
Sound score	Milo Kossowski
Lighting	Rose Connors Dance
Photography	Gregory Lorenzutti

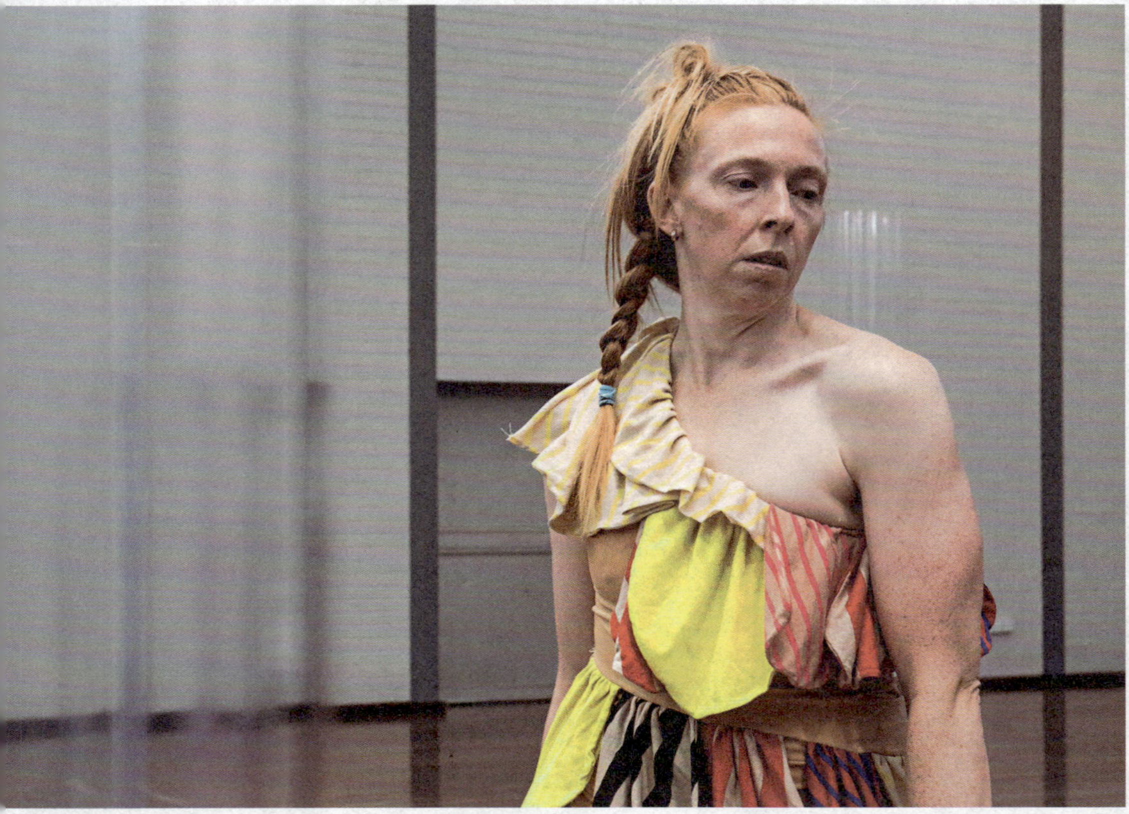

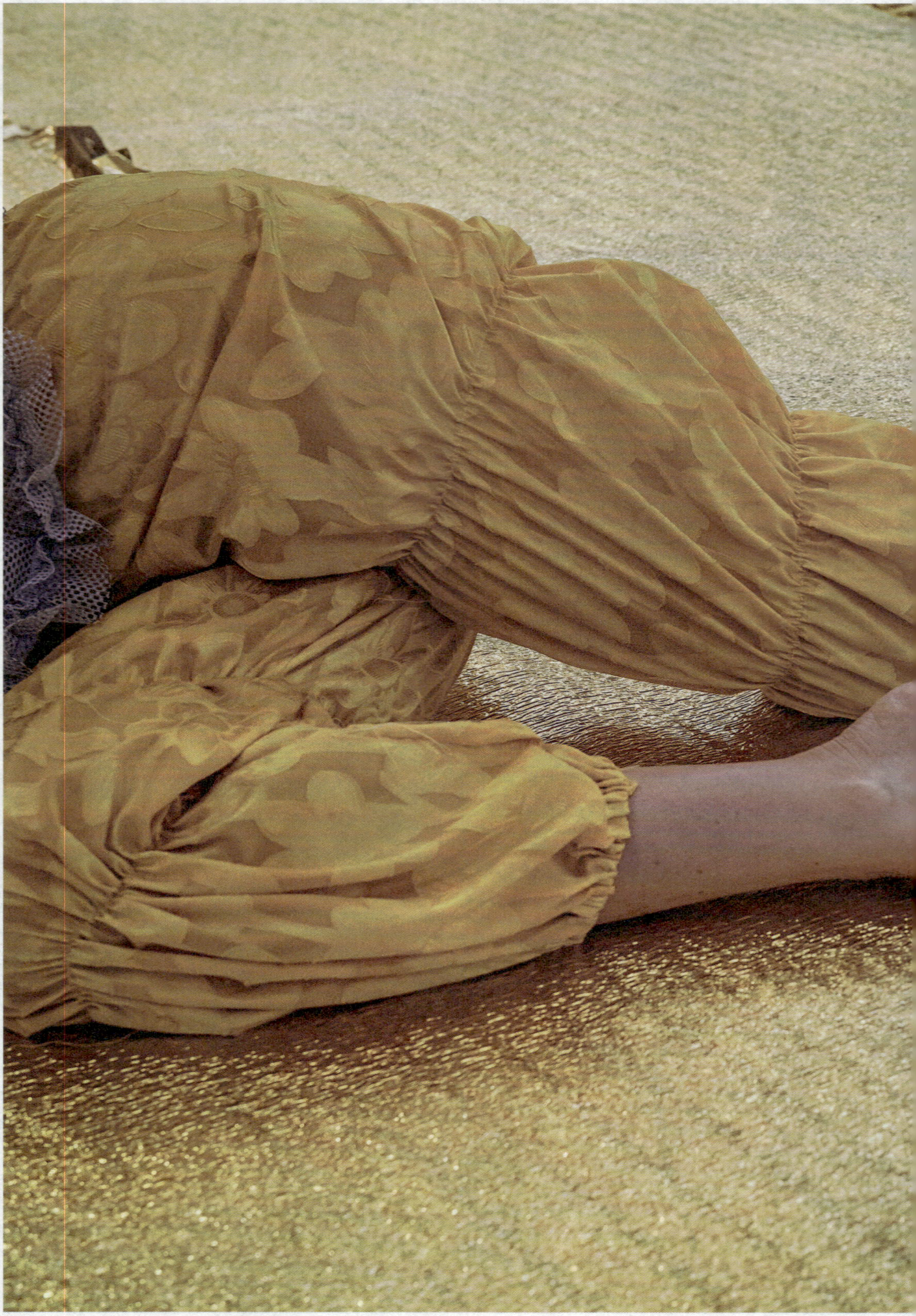

ACROMAT

How Choreography Works 460–465 L1
by Shelley Lasica, Deanne Butterworth and Jo Lloyd

Medium	exhibition and ensemble performance
Venue	West Space, Melbourne
Dates	9 October, 24 October, 6–7 November 2015
Performers	Deanne Butterworth Shelley Lasica (primary performer) Jo Lloyd
Photography	Christo Crocker
Producer	Kara Ward
Archival video selection	Deanne Butterworth Jo Lloyd
Video editing	Duane Morrison
Object	Shelley Lasica (design) Tom Burless (fabrication)

How How Choreography Works 467–478 L2
by Shelley Lasica, Deanne Butterworth and Jo Lloyd

Medium	ensemble performance
Venue	Art Gallery of New South Wales, Sydney
Date	27 April 2016
Event	Choreography and the Gallery, curated by Erin Brannigan and presented by the 20th Biennale of Sydney and UNSW Sydney
Performers	Deanne Butterworth Shelley Lasica Jo Lloyd
Producers	Melissa Ratliff Sarah Rodigari
Videography	Samuel James
Pictured	museum angle barriers from Helen Grogan (assisted by Geoff Robinson), OBSTRUCTION DRIFT (AGNSW) 2016

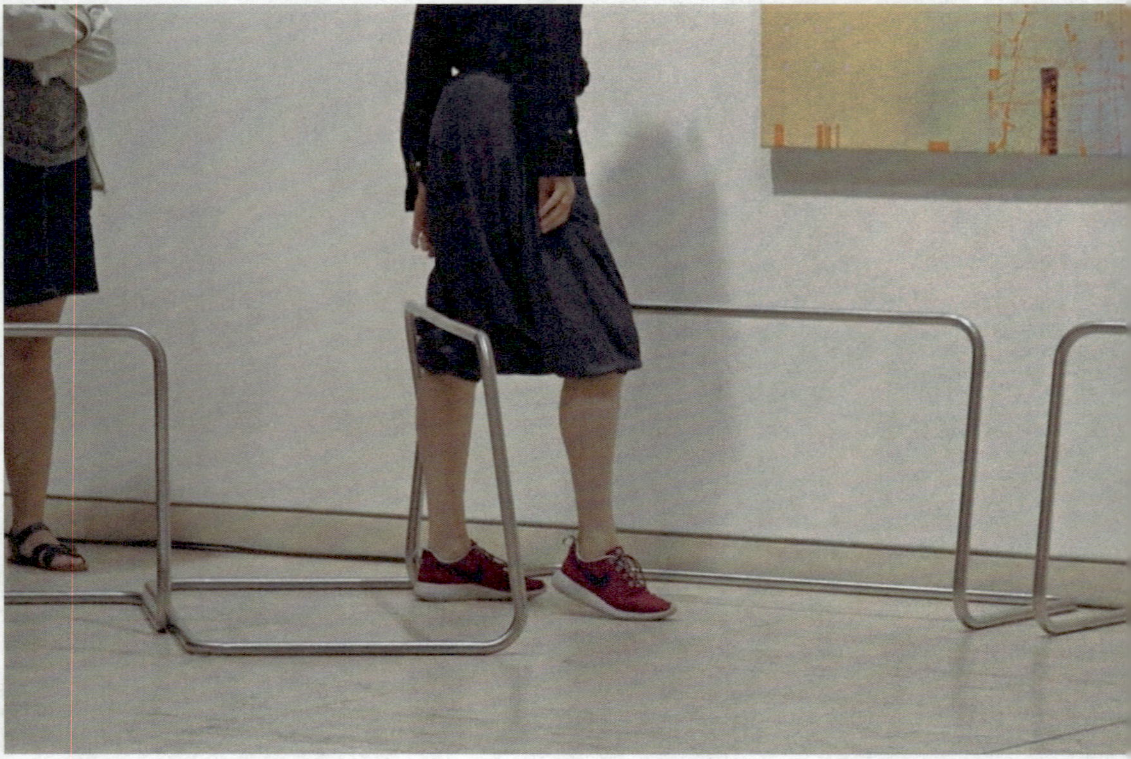

The Shape of Things to Come
The Design Plot
Greater Union
If I Don’t Understand You
WHEN I AM NOT THERE

he Shape of Things to Come 485–491 **M1**

Medium	**solo performance**
Venue	**The Hotel Windsor, Melbourne**
Dates	**18–21 August 2016**
Event	**Room 301 at SPRING 1883, performance series curated by Mark Feary**
Original title	**To Be Moved**
Producer	**Zoe Theodore**
Costume	**Belinda Hellier**
Photography	**Mark Feary**

he Shape of Things to Come 492–509 **M2**

Medium	**solo performance**
Venue	**Artspace, Sydney**
Date	**9 February 2017**
Event	**Superposition of Three Types, 9 February – 17 April 2017**
Producer	**Zoe Theodore**
Costume	**Belinda Hellier**
Photography	**Jessica Maurer**

'he Design Plot 515–527 N1

Medium	durational ensemble performance
Venue	Gertrude Glasshouse, Melbourne
Dates	23 February – 4 March 2017
Performers	Ellen Davies Timothy Harvey Louella May Hogan Shelley Lasica Daniel Newell Lilian Steiner Jo White
Producer	Zoe Theodore
Wardrobe	Shelley Lasica
Photography	Sarah Walker

'he Design Plot 529–547 N2

Medium	video based on the performance staged at the Royal Melbourne Tennis Club, Melbourne
Year	2017
Duration	49 minutes
Performers	Ellen Davies Timothy Harvey Louella May Hogan Shelley Lasica Daniel Newell Lilian Steiner Jo White
Director and editor	James Wright
Camera	James Wright Eugene Perepletchikov
Sound recordist	Benjamin Walbrook
Wardrobe	Shelley Lasica
Producer	Zoe Theodore

he Design Plot 549–558 **N3**

Medium	durational ensemble performance
Venue	MPavilion, Melbourne
Date	4 February 2018
Performers	Ellen Davies Timothy Harvey Louella May Hogan Shelley Lasica Daniel Newell Lilian Steiner Jo White
Producer	Zoe Theodore
Wardrobe	Shelley Lasica
Photography	Jacqui Shelton

he Design Plot 561–576 **N4**

Medium	durational ensemble performance
Venue	215 Albion Street, Brunswick, Melbourne
Date	12 July 2018
Performers	Ellen Davies Timothy Harvey Louella May Hogan Shelley Lasica Daniel Newell Lilian Steiner Jo White
Producer	Zoe Theodore
Wardrobe	Shelley Lasica
Photography	Jacqui Shelton

he Design Plot 578–595 **N5**

Medium	ensemble performance
Venue	Immigration Museum, Melbourne
Date	9 February 2020
Event	Curated by Amrita Hepi and Zoe Theodore for the Summer of Dance series, 2019–20
Performers	Ellen Davies Timothy Harvey Shelley Lasica Daniel Newell Lilian Steiner Jo White
Producer	Zoe Theodore
Wardrobe	Shelley Lasica
Photography	Jacqui Shelton

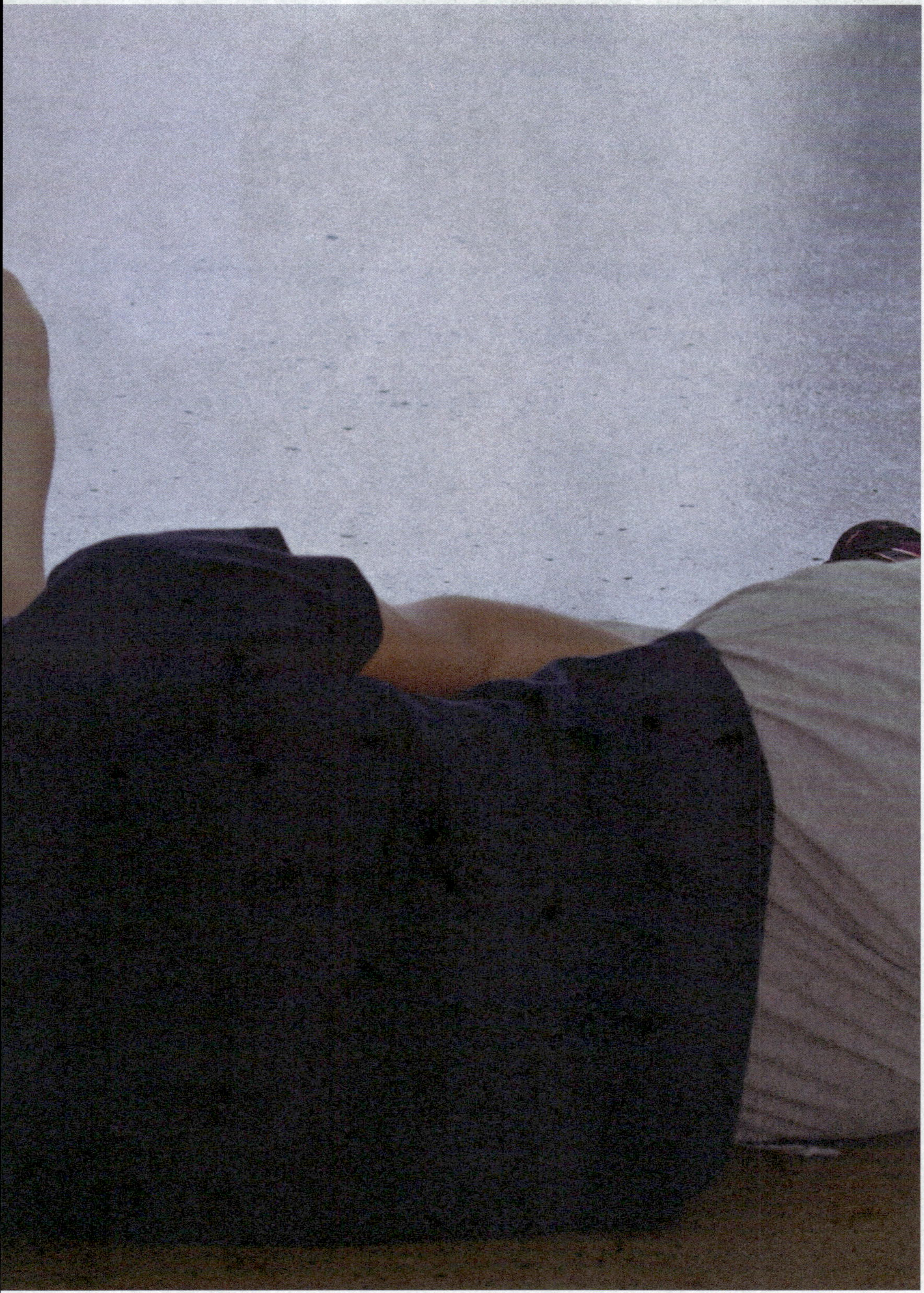

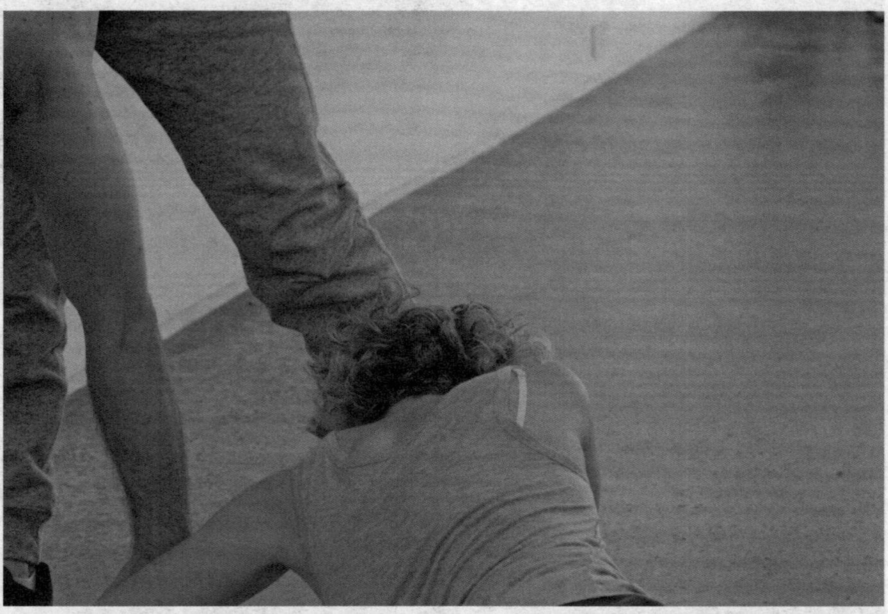

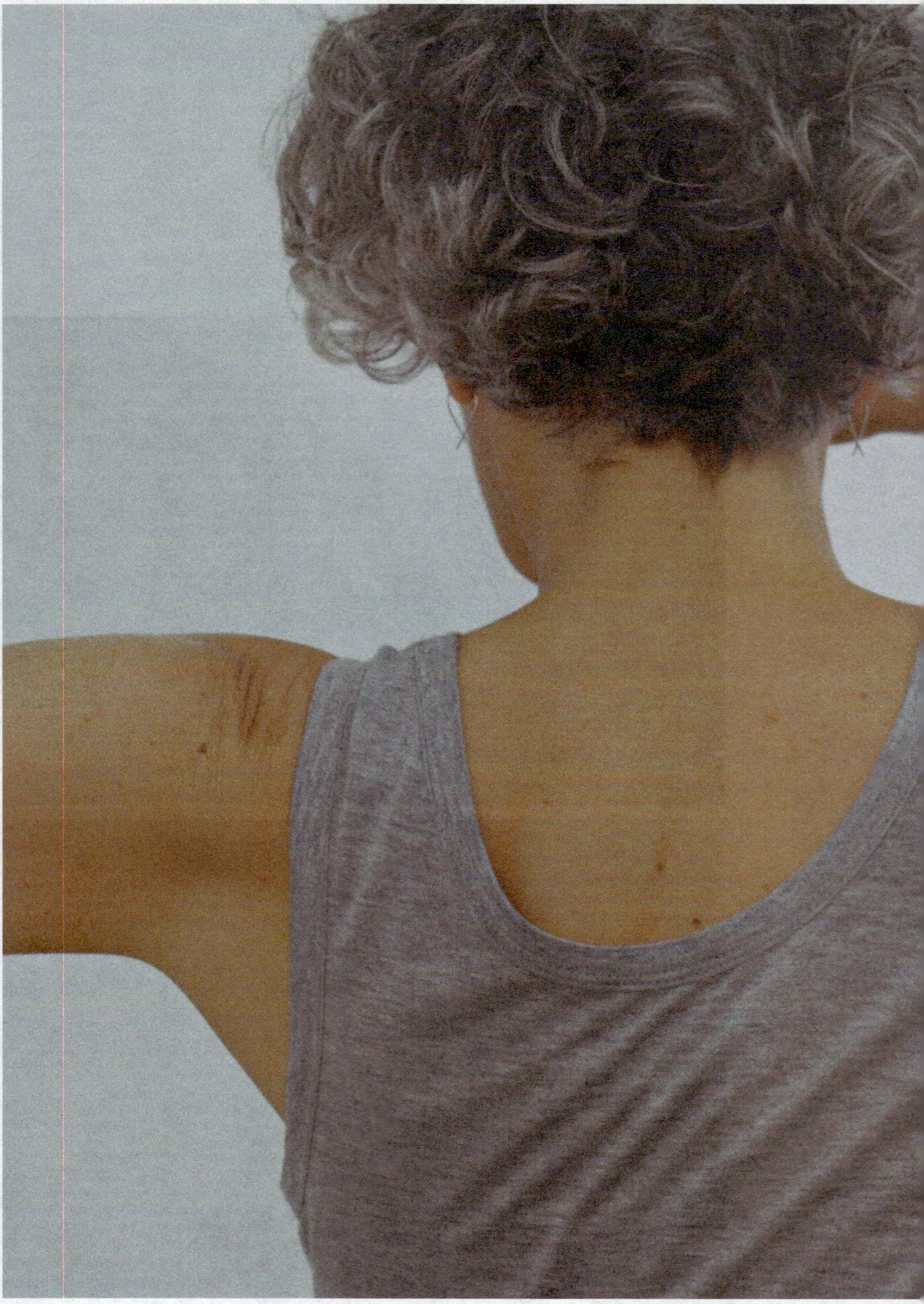

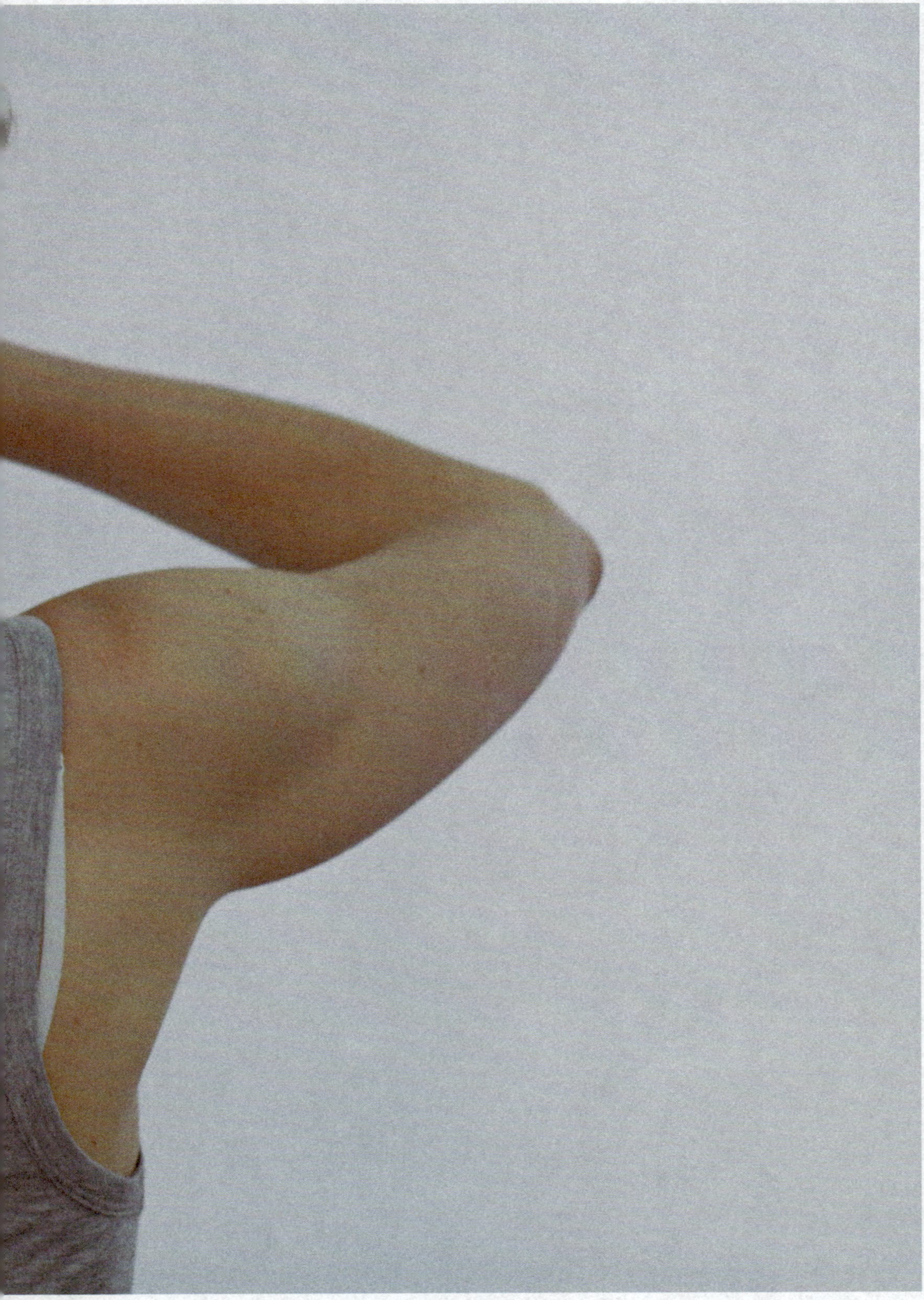

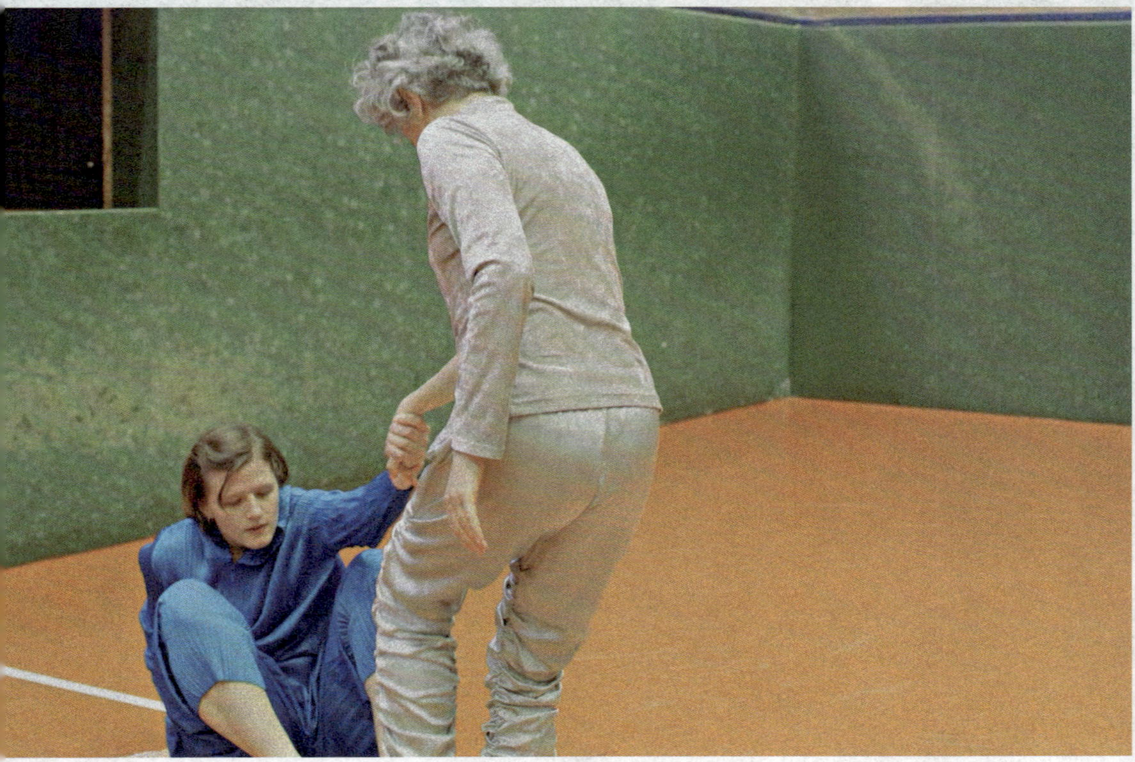

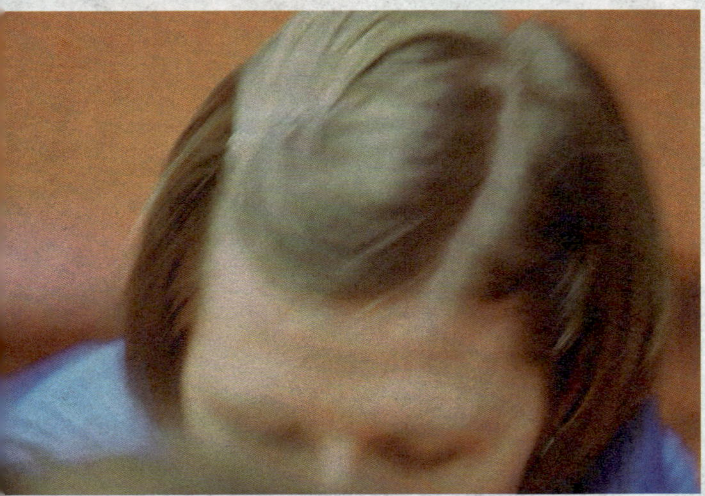

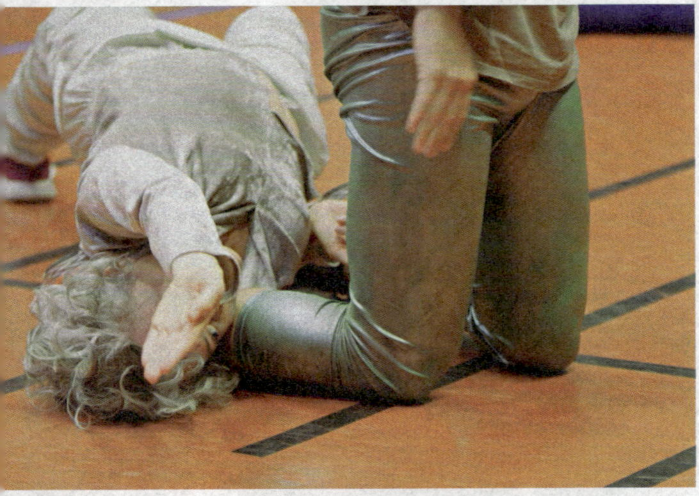

enduraflex

enduraflex
enduraflex
enduraflex

Fire Stairs

JUST DO IT.

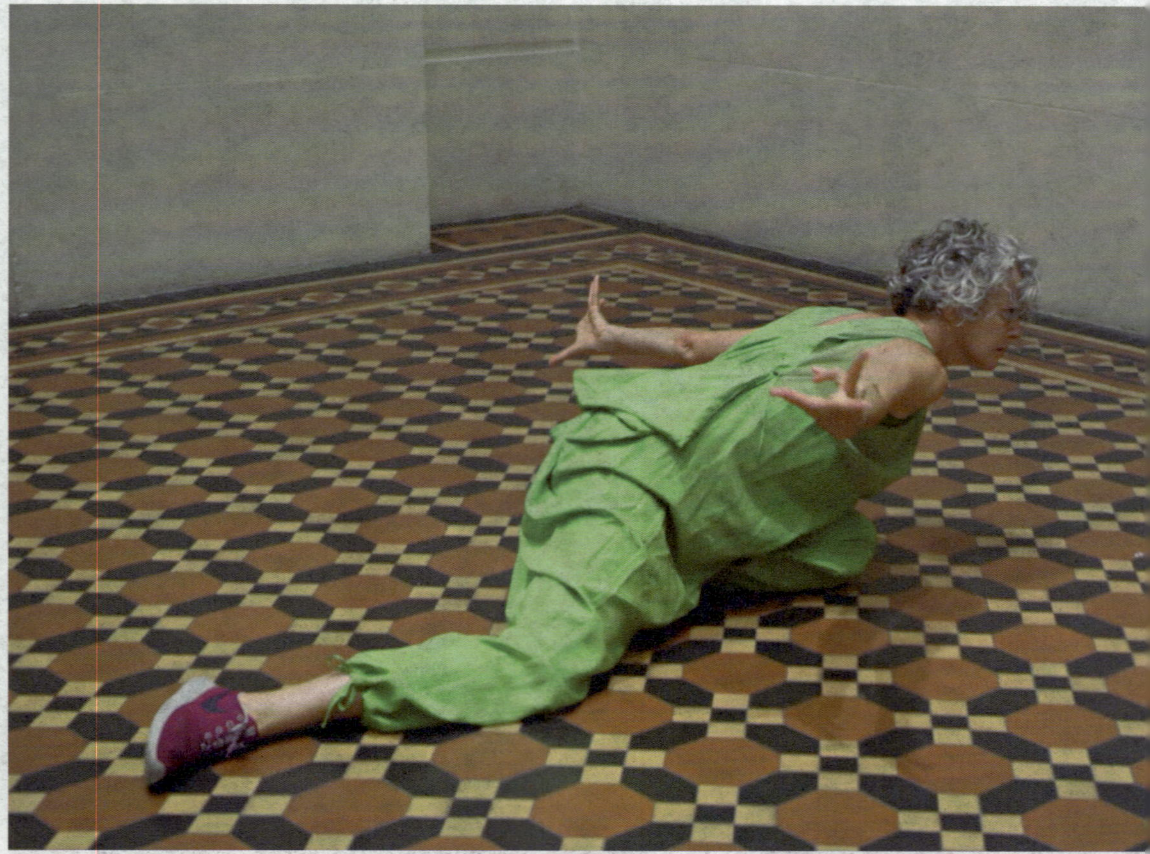

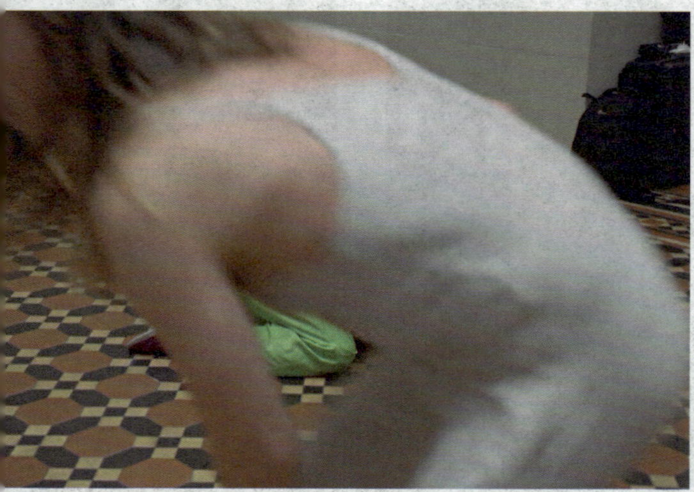

Fire Stairs
Use only in case
of emergency
Fire Stairs
Use only in case
of emergency

Medium	durational duet performance
Venue	215 Albion Street, Brunswick, Melbourne
Date	21 October 2018
Event	TO DO / TO MAKE 2, curated by Shelley Lasica and Zoe Theodore in association with Neon Parc
Performers	Timothy Harvey Shelley Lasica
Video projection	Callum Morton (originally produced for RESTRICTED SITUATION 1999)
Objects	Anne-Marie May (originally produced for VIANNE 2008)
Producer	Zoe Theodore
Photography	Jacqui Shelton
Pictured	red rope from Brooke Stamp and Sidney McMahon, an enactment of its own (burning) poetics 2018

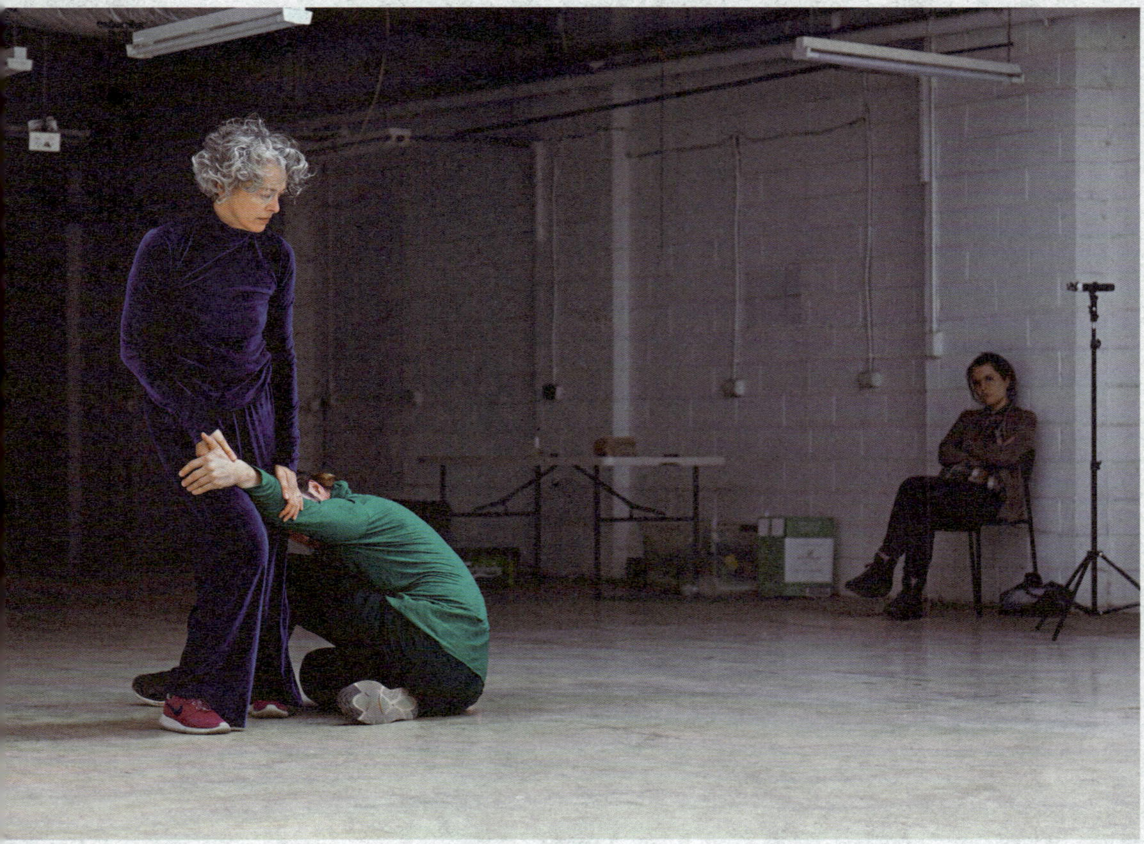

EMERGENCY
EXIT ONLY

Medium	ensemble performance
Venue	Neon Parc, Melbourne
Date	5 December 2019
Performers	LJ Connolly-Hiatt
	Luke Fryer
	Shelley Lasica
	Megan Payne
	Lana Šprajcer
Producer	Zoe Theodore
Mise-en-scène	Colby Vexler
Sound score	Milo Kossowski
Wardrobe	Shelley Lasica
Photography	Rudi Williams

PARIS

adidas

PARIS

Medium	ensemble performance with sound, costumes, nautical net, movable screen and a selection of existing contributions from others
Venues	Monash University Museum of Art, Melbourne and Art Gallery of New South Wales, Sydney
Dates	16–27 August 2022 and May 2023
Event	Shelley Lasica: WHEN I AM NOT THERE, performance-exhibition curated by Hannah Mathews
Performers	LJ Connolly-Hiatt Luke Fryer Timothy Harvey Rebecca Jensen Shelley Lasica Megan Payne Oliver Savariego Lana Šprajcer
Creative producer	Zoe Theodore
Consultants	Lisa Radford Colby Vexler
Sound score	François Tétaz (composition) from scores by François Tétaz and Milo Kossowski commissioned for earlier works by Shelley Lasica
Photography	rehearsal images by Jacqui Shelton at Princes Park; Monash Art, Design and Architecture; Abbotsford Convent (all Melbourne)

Q

SHELLEY LASICA is based in Naarm/Melbourne and has been working nationally and internationally for over four decades. Her practice has consistently engaged with the contexts and situations of presenting dance, choreography and performance. Interested in the collective and interdisciplinary possibilities of choreography, she performs her solo and ensemble works in dialogue with designers, writers and visual artists. Lasica's choreographic works have been shown within visual art, theatre and festival contexts. These include the Melbourne Festival; National Gallery of Victoria, Melbourne; Chunky Move, Melbourne; Gertrude Contemporary, Melbourne; Artspace, Sydney; Centre nationale de la danse, Paris; Siobhan Davies Studios, London; Dance Massive, Melbourne; Australian Centre for Contemporary Art, Melbourne; and Anna Schwartz Gallery, Melbourne. Presenting work in indeterminate spaces is also an integral part of her choreographic practice. Throughout her career, Lasica has organised and participated in numerous residencies, exchanges and mentorship programs in Australia and overseas. She teaches choreography to dance and visual arts students both independently and within institutions.

BIOGRAPHY

1977–1982 Member, Modern Dance Ensemble, Melbourne

1982 Research assistant, George Paton Gallery, University of Melbourne

1982–1984 Teaches movement as part of the Activities program run by the University of Melbourne Student Union

1983–1984 Studies dance with Margaret Lasica and others in Australia, including Pauline de Groot, Russell Dumas, Eva Karczag, Lisa Kraus, Christine Mearing and Dana Reitz

1984 Co-founds Independent Dance Artists (IDA) with Eleanor Brickhill and Felicity MacDonald; Lucy Guerin and Sandra Parker join later.

1984–1987 Writes articles on dance for *NMA*, *Writings on Dance*, *Tension*, *Lowdown*, *Spectator Burns* and the University of Melbourne student paper, *Farrago*

1984–1985 Gallery assistant, Christine Abrahams Gallery, Melbourne

1985 Completes a Bachelor of Fine Arts, University of Melbourne. Commences a Bachelor of Arts (Dance) at Adelaide College of the Arts and Education but withdraws shortly after.

CHRONOLOGY OF WORKS

1983 Title not recorded
solo performance
Extensions, Melbourne
Presented as part of Image '83

1984 *Appearing to Create Something Solid*
solo performance
Extensions, Melbourne, 28 Jul and 4 Aug
Presented as part of Dance '84, 26 Jul – 11 Aug
Costumes—Margaret Lasica

1985 *Without Breaking Through, Seeing Is Believing*
solo performance
Extensions, Melbourne
Presented as part of Image '85

1986 *Describing the perspective of time, It promises you nothing*
solo performance
Reconnaissance Gallery, Melbourne, 5–7 Sep
Costumes—Martin Grant and Fiona Scanlan
Lighting—Roger Wood

1987 *Sights and Vision*
solo performance
Australian Centre for Contemporary Art, Melbourne, 4 Apr
Presented as part of the performance art program *Evenings without Andy Warhol*, 2–12 Apr

1987 *Turning Away the Affect of a Mystery*
solo performance
Athenaeum Theatre 2, Melbourne, 6–9 Aug and Performance Space, Sydney, Nov
Set and objects—Roger Wood
Costumes—Martin Grant and Fiona Scanlan
Lighting—Nathan Thompson

1988 Six-month residency, 200 Gertrude Street, Melbourne

1988 Participates in the Australia and New Zealand Bicentennial Dance Course, directed by David Gordon, with his Pick Up Performance Company in residence

1988 *Variations from Verisimilitude, No. 1, 2, 3*
solo performance
Australian Centre for Contemporary Art, Melbourne, 10–11 Sep

1988 *Turning Away the Affect of a Mystery*
video documentation presented at Inflation Nightclub, Melbourne, 18 Sep
Performer—Shelley Lasica
Costumes—Martin Grant and Fiona Scanlan
Lighting—Roger Wood

1988 *Variations from Verisimilitude, No. 1, 2, 3, 4, 5*
solo, duet and trio performances
The Edge, Sydney, 8–9 Oct
Performers—Shelley Lasica; Lasica and Felicity MacDonald; Lasica, MacDonald and Eleanor Brickhill

1988 *Variations from Verisimilitude, No. 2, 3, 4, 5*
solo, duet and trio performances
200 Gertrude Street, Melbourne, 15–16 Oct
Performers—Shelley Lasica; Lasica and Felicity MacDonald; Lasica, MacDonald and Eleanor Brickhill

1988 *Verisimilitude*
solo performance
Performance Space 122, New York City, 2–4 Dec
Presented as part of New Stuff Season

1989 Gertrude studio artist, Gertrude Residency Program, Melbourne

1989 Curator of *Physical Culture*, an exhibition, lecture and seminar series on contemporary dance at 200 Gertrude Street, Melbourne.
Artists—Teresa Blake, Stephen Bram, Andrew Browne, Aleks Danko, John De Silentio, Louise Forthun, Mutlu Hassan, Shelley Lasica, Melbourne Research Group, Elizabeth Newman, Trevor Patrick, Rosslynd Piggott, Sarah Ritson, Jacqui Rutten, Shiralee Saul, Richard Todd, Dan Wilton

1989 *Now*
solo performance
City Gallery, Melbourne, 30 Nov – 2 Dec
Set design—Roger Wood
Paper text artworks—Shiralee Saul
Video—Sylvie Mackie
Costume—Fiona Scanlan
Music—Toshiro Mayuzumi, Maurice Ravel, Jeff Beck, Madonna

1990 *Now*
solo performance
Performance Space, Sydney, 5–8 Apr
Set design—Roger Wood
Paper text artworks—Shiralee Saul
Video—Sylvie Mackie
Costume—Fiona Scanlan
Music—Toshiro Mayuzumi, Maurice Ravel, Jeff Beck, Madonna

1990 *Now*
solo performance
The Place Theatre, London, 4–5 May
Presented as part of The Turning World International Dance Festival
Set design—Roger Wood
Paper text artworks—Shiralee Saul
Video—Sylvie Mackie
Costume—Fiona Scanlan
Music—Toshiro Mayuzumi, Maurice Ravel, Jeff Beck, Madonna

1991 Performs in Gaby Agis's work at Chisenhale Gallery, London, 9–12 Oct
Presented as part of Dance Umbrella festival, in association with the solo exhibition by Cornelia Parker, *Cold Dark Matter: An Exploded View*, 18 Sep – 27 Oct

1993 Contributes choreography and performance to *Oresteia*, an opera for 6 voices, 11 instruments and dancer
Theatreworks, Melbourne, premiering 16 May (14 performances)
Presented by ELISION
Libretto—Liza Lim and Barrie Kosky
Director—Barrie Kosky
Conductor—Sandro Gorli
Stage designer—Peter Corrigan
Choreography/performance—Shelley Lasica

1990 *You*
solo performance
Interim Art (later Maureen Paley), London, 6 May
Video—Sylvie Mackie

1990 Title not recorded
solo performance
Extensions, Melbourne
Presented as part of IMAGE '90, Jun and Jul

1990 *BELIEVE*
solo performance
City Gallery, Melbourne, 30 Nov, 1–2 Dec
Set design—Roger Wood
Scenery—Tony Clark

1991 *BELIEVE*
solo performance
Yuill|Crowley Gallery, Sydney, 19–21 Feb
Set design—Roger Wood
Scenery—Tony Clark

1991 Gaby Agis and Shelley Lasica
Title not recorded
duet performance
Interim Art (later Maureen Paley), London, 16 May; Chisenhale Dance Space, London, 17 May
Performers—Gaby Agis and Shelley Lasica

1991 *Happening Simultaneously*
solo performance
City Gallery, Melbourne, 17–20 Dec
Design—Roger Wood
Stage manager—Sarah Halls
Communications design—Ian Robertson
Publicity images—Hugo Glendinning

1992 With Wendy Lasica, brings dance artists to Australia to teach and perform: David Dorfman, Lance Gries, Julyen Hamilton, Wendy Houston, Iréne Hultman, Bebe Miller, Jennifer Monson, Lloyd Newson and Stephen Petronio. Activities take place at Extensions dance studio in Carlton and various locations around Australia.

1992 *Happening*
solo performance
Store 5, Melbourne, 26–28 Nov, 3–5 Dec

1993 With Roger Wood, conducts workshop 'What Is this Thing Called Dancing?' for Physical State International's autumn season of performing arts training, 9 Oct, The Green Room, Manchester, England

1993 Runs Extensions, the Carlton dance studio originally set up by Margaret Lasica

1993 *Temporal*
duet performance
185 Flinders Lane, Melbourne, 25–28 Mar, 1–4 Apr
Performers—Shelley Lasica and Sandra Parker
Sculpture—Gail Hastings

1993 *TRIPLEX* (including *Disappear*, *BELIEVE* and *Happening Simultaneously*)
solo performance
Institute of Modern Art, Brisbane, 24–26 Jun
Set design—Roger Wood
Scenery—Tony Clark
Lighting—Roger Wood
Projection—Gail Hastings

1998 Bal [illegible]
solo performance
[illegible] Arts [illegible] Cafe, London, [illegible] May
Music—Sylvie [illegible]

1999 Title not recorded
solo performance
[illegible] Melbourne
Presented as part of [illegible] of DIAF

2000 solo performance
City [illegible], Melbourne, 30 Nov–1 Dec
Set design—Roger Wood
Sound—Tony Clark

1998 BREATHE
solo performance
[illegible] Gallery, Sydney, [illegible]
Set design—Roger Wood
Sound—Tony Clark

2000 Cathy Arts and Shelley Lasica
Title not recorded
duet performance
Interim [illegible], London
New Crossing Dance [illegible], London, 12 May
Performers—Cathy [illegible] and Shelley Lasica
[illegible]

2001 solo performance
City Gallery, Melbourne, [illegible] Dec
Design—Roger Wood
[illegible]—Sarah [illegible]
[illegible]—Ian [illegible]
[illegible]—Hugo [illegible]

1991 [illegible]
solo performance
[illegible], Melbourne, 26 Nov–1 Dec

1992 [illegible]
duet performance
[illegible], Melbourne
[illegible] Apr
Performers—Shelley Lasica and [illegible] Barker
Sound—[illegible] Hastings

1993 [illegible] Concluding [illegible]
[illegible]
solo performance
Institute of Modern Art, Brisbane, 24 [illegible]
Design—Roger Wood
Sound—Tony Clark
Lighting—[illegible]
Production—[illegible] Hastings

1997 With Wendy Lasica, a free dance artist, to Australia to teach and perform with David Dorfman, [illegible], Janet Hamilton, Wendy Houstoun, Jorge Holmes, [illegible], Margaret Ivinson, Claudia [illegible] and Stephen Petronio. Activities take place at [illegible] dance studios in Carlton and various locations around Australia.

1993 With Roger Wood, conducts workshop 'What is this thing Called Dancing?' for [illegible] State International [illegible] performing arts training [illegible]. The [illegible], England.

1994 [illegible], the Gertrude Street [illegible] [illegible] by Margaret Lasica

1993 *TRIPLEX* (including *Disappear*, *BELIEVE* and *Happening Simultaneously*)
solo performance
Perth Institute of Contemporary Arts, Perth, 22–24 Jul
Set design—Roger Wood
Scenery—Tony Clark
Lighting—Roger Wood
Projection—Gail Hastings

1993 *TRIPLEX* (including *Disappear*, *BELIEVE* and *Happening Simultaneously*)
solo performance
The Green Room, Manchester, England, 9–10 Oct
Producer—Warren G. Pringle
Projection—Gail Hastings

1993 *TRIPLEX* (including *Disappear*, *BELIEVE* and *Happening Simultaneously*)
solo performance
The Hacienda, Manchester, England, 11 Oct
Producer—Warren G. Pringle
Projection—Gail Hastings

1993 *TRIPLEX* (including *Disappear*, *BELIEVE* and *Happening Simultaneously*)
solo performance
The Cornerhouse, Manchester, England, 12 Oct
Producer—Warren G. Pringle
Set design—Roger Wood
Scenery—Tony Clark
Projection—Gail Hastings

1993 *BEHAVIOUR Part 1*
solo performance
Store 5, Melbourne, 24–28 Nov

1994 Participates in the group exhibition *Projection: Filming the Body*, The Basement Project, Melbourne

1994 *BEHAVIOUR Part 1 and 2*
solo performance
Athenaeum Theatre and Anna Schwartz Gallery, Melbourne, 5–7 May; Performance Space, Sydney, 31 May and 3 Jun; Yuill|Crowley Gallery, Sydney, 1–2 Jun; and Experimental Art Foundation, Adelaide

1994 *BEHAVIOUR Part 5*
solo performance
Southbank Centre, London, 10 Sep
Presented as part of *Rhythm Method*
Music composition/live music—Laurence Crane

1994 Title not recorded
ensemble performance
Extensions, Melbourne, 17 Dec
Presented as part of *Christmas Pageant*
Performers—Shelley Lasica, Trevor Patrick, Sandra Parker, John Utans, Ros Warby

1994 Margie Medlin, *BEHAVIOUR* 1994
video based on the solo performance by Shelley Lasica at Store 5, 1993; 12 minutes
Presented in 1994 at the Australian Centre for Contemporary Art, Melbourne, and Women in Film, Sydney; and as part of *Body of Work: Australia*, Reel Dance, 11 Oct 2003
Performer—Shelley Lasica
Sound design—Dan Witton

1996 Performs in Lyndal Jones, *Spitfire 1 2 3* 1996
multimedia performance
Lonsdale Street Power Station, Melbourne, 10–27 Apr
Performers—Nadja Kostich, Deanne Flatley, Helen Hopkins, Shelley Lasica, Rhys Muldoon, Boris Rotar, Michael Sheridan, Bryan Smith, Miliana Cancar
Music—David Chesworth
Lighting—Margie Medlin

1996 Performs in Bryan Smith, *Sexed* 1996
ensemble performance
Malthouse Theatre, Melbourne, 13 Jul
Choreography—Bryan Smith
Scenography and costumes—Ben Anderson
Presented for the Green Mill Dance Project festival, *World Dance*, 1–20 Jul

1995 *Here BEHAVIOUR Part 4*
solo performance
Anna Schwartz Gallery, Melbourne, 11–14 May, and in the same year at Institute of Modern Art, Brisbane; Experimental Art Foundation, Adelaide

1995 *Becoming Solid*
solos and duet performance
Perth Institute of Contemporary Arts, Perth
Performers—Shelley Lasica and Sandra Parker

1996

1996 *CHARACTER X*
ensemble performance
Fitzroy Town Hall, Melbourne, 23 May – 1 Jun
Presented as part of Next Wave Festival
Performers—Deanne Butterworth, Shelley Lasica, Carlee Mellow, Sandra Parker, Kylie Walters
Construction and lighting design—Roger Wood
Costumier and visual design—Kathy Temin
Composer—Paul Schütze
Lighting consultant—Hamish Inglis
Stage manager—Elizabeth Keen
Postcard design—Yanni Florence
Publicity images—Polly Borland
Project management—Wendy Lasica

1996 *Square Dance BEHAVIOUR Part 6*
solo performance
Australia House, London, 19 Sep

1996 *BEHAVIOUR Part 1*
solo performance
T-Junction, Museumsquartier, Vienna, 30 Sep

1996 *BEHAVIOUR Part 1*
solo performance
Private studio, New York City, in a series curated by Lance Gries

1996 *Square Dance BEHAVIOUR Part 6*
solo performance
Anna Schwartz Gallery, Melbourne, 5–8 Dec

1997

1997 With Wendy Lasica, conceives the international exchange project *SPAN*, involving the visit of international artists Susan Braham and Bebe Miller to Australia, and performances by Shelley Lasica and Sandra Parker in New York City

1997 *Square Dance BEHAVIOUR Part 6*
solo performance
Performance Space, Sydney, Mar
Presented as part of *antistatic* festival, 21 Mar – 4 Apr

1997 *live drama situation*
solo performance
Cleveland, London, 27 May

1997 Susan Braham, Shelley Lasica, Bebe Miller and Sandra Parker
Another Place
ensemble performance
Danspace, St Mark's Church and Wave Hill, New York, 9 and 13 Jul
Performers—Susan Braham, Shelley Lasica, Bebe Miller, Sandra Parker
Music—Guy Klucevsek, played by Anne DeMarinis and the composer
Presented as part of *SPAN*, an international exchange project developed by Shelley and Wendy Lasica

1998 Assistant director for *JET LAG*,
cross-media performance project
by The Builders Association and Diller + Scofidio,
directed by Marianne Weems and touring
1998–2000 to multiple venues in Europe and
the United States

1998 Performs in theatre pieces *Evidence*,
Monologues and *Sleepers* directed by
James Clayden, La Mama, Melbourne

1999

1997 *SITUATION LIVE: THE SUBJECT*
duet performance
La Mama, Melbourne, 12–23 Nov
Performers—Deanne Butterworth, Jo Lloyd
Stage manager—Elizabeth Keen
Script—Robyn McKenzie
Costumes—Shelley Lasica (concept), Shio Otani (design)
Music composition—François Tétaz

1998 Collaborates with Kara Baker on PROJECT, a fashion house represented in the collection of the National Gallery of Victoria, Melbourne

1998 Shelley Lasica with Martin Grant
DRESS
solo performance, 25 minutes
Anna Schwartz Gallery, Melbourne, 12–15 Feb, in association with the Woolmark Melbourne Fashion Festival; Performance Space, Sydney, 15–18 Apr, including a performance of *SITUATION LIVE: THE SUBJECT*
Costume—Martin Grant

1998 *SITUATION LIVE: THE SUBJECT*
duet performance
Australian Centre for Contemporary Art, 22 Apr
Performers—Deanne Butterworth, Jo Lloyd
Script—Robyn McKenzie
Costumes—Shelley Lasica (concept), Shio Otani (design)
Music composition—François Tétaz

1998 *LIVE OPERA SITUATION*
ensemble performance
Wesleyan Hall, Albert Park, Melbourne, 15–18, 21–25 Jul
Presented as part of *DW98*, commissioned by Dance Works
Performers—Belinda Cooper, Jo Lloyd, Carlee Mellow, Rachel Roberts
Costumes—Shelley Lasica
Sound score—François Tétaz

1999 Further research period for the project *SPAN*, with artists Susan Braham, Bebe Miller and Sandra Parker, and videography by Ben Speth

1999 *ACTION SITUATION*
trio performance
East Wing Gallery, Immigration Museum, Melbourne, 12–14, 18–20 Feb
Performers—Deanne Butterworth, Jo Lloyd, Kylie Walters
Script—Robyn McKenzie
Costumes—Kara Baker and Shelley Lasica for PROJECT
Sound score—François Tétaz
Lighting—John Ford

1999 *ACTION SITUATION*
trio performance
Performance Space, Sydney, 24–28 Aug
Presented as part of *Australian Perspecta 99: Living Here Now—Art and Politics*
Performers—Deanne Butterworth, Jo Lloyd, Deborah Saxon
Script—Robyn McKenzie
Costumes—Kara Baker and Shelley Lasica for PROJECT
Sound score—François Tétaz
Lighting—John Ford

2001 Performs in *Teorema*, an opera without singing based on a film by Pier Paolo Pasolini
Merlyn Theatre, Malthouse, Melbourne, 9–12 Aug
Presented by Chamber Made
Composer—Giorgio Battistelli
Director—Douglas Horton
Music direction—Roland Peelman
Design—Peter Corrigan
Performers—Michele Heaven, Juan Jackson, Shelley Lasica, Barbara Sambell, Ian Scott, Tom Wright

2003 Contributes choreography to Fiona Macdonald, *Museum Emotions* 2003
digital betacam video, 104 minutes
Cast—Sarah Berner, Jon Campbell, Andrea Carbone, Justin Clemens, Travis de Jong, Max Delany, Tim Harvey, Trudy Hellier, Craig Judd, Milo Kossowski, Brendan Lee, Rachel Meisner, Amanda Morgan, Callum Morton, Jacqueline Riva, Scott Robinson, Justin Schmidt, Jason Smith, Masato Takasaka, Ronnie van Hout, Lyndal Walker, Constanze Zikos
Dancers—Deanne Butterworth, Jacob Lehrer, Jo Lloyd
Producer—Fiona Macdonald and Froth Productions
Choreography—Shelley Lasica
Score—Chris Henschke, Ben Harper, Michael Munson

2003 Performs in producer, director, writer and editor James Clayden's film *Hamlet X*, part of Clayden's *The Ghost Paintings* series of short films

1999 *RESTRICTED SITUATION*
ensemble performance
Presented by Chunky Move as part of *Live Acts #1*, Revolver, Melbourne, 22–25 Sep
Performers—Luke Smiles, Fiona Cameron, Byron Perry
Video projection—Callum Morton
Sound score—François Tétaz

2002 Devises and leads the project *Plan Protean*, a pedagogical model used to develop *Solos Project Retrospective* and *Play in a Room*, among other works

2002 *History Situation*
ensemble performance
Horti Hall, Melbourne, 14–17, 21–24 Mar
Presented as part of the L'Oréal Melbourne Fashion Festival
Performers—Deanne Butterworth, Timothy Harvey, Jacob Lehrer, Jo Lloyd, Bronwyn Ritchie
Video—Ben Speth
Backdrop—Roger Wood
Script—Robyn McKenzie
Costumes—Richard Nylon
Sound score—François Tétaz
Lighting—Roger Wood
Invitation—Daniel von Sturmer

2003 Residency, Tower Studio, Queens College, University of Melbourne

2003 *Solos Project*
ensemble performance
The Ian Potter Centre: NGV Australia and Anna Schwartz Gallery, Melbourne, 1 Mar
Performers—Deanne Butterworth, Timothy Harvey, Shelley Lasica, Jacob Lehrer, Jo Lloyd, Bronwyn Ritchie, Julia Robinson
Costumes—Shelley Lasica

2003 *Play in a Room*
ensemble performance
Tower Studio, Queens College, University of Melbourne, Melbourne, 4–7 Dec
Performers—Deanne Butterworth, Timothy Harvey, Shelley Lasica, Jacob Lehrer, Jo Lloyd, Bronwyn Ritchie, Julia Robinson
Costumes—Kara Baker and Shelley Lasica for PROJECT

2004 *SET UP/SITUATION LIVE*
duet performance
State Theatre Company of South Australia rehearsal room, Adelaide Festival Centre, Adelaide, 25–26 Feb
Presented independently alongside APAM (Australian Performing Arts Market), the Australia Council's biennial showcase event
Performers—Deanne Butterworth, Timothy Harvey
Sound score—François Tétaz

2005 *Play in a Room*
ensemble performance, 2 sessions, 45 minutes
State Theatre Rehearsal Room, Arts Centre, Melbourne, 16 Oct
Presented as part of the Melbourne International Arts Festival
Performers—Kristy Ayre, Deanne Butterworth, Luke George, Timothy Harvey, Kyle Kremerskothen, Shelley Lasica, Jacob Lehrer, Jo Lloyd, Daina Pjekne, Bronwyn Ritchie, Julia Robinson, Brooke Stamp
Costumes—Shelley Lasica
Sound score—François Tétaz (music originally composed for *History Situation* 2002 and remixed for *Play in a Room*)

2006 Residency, Centre national de la danse, Paris (with Deanne Butterworth and Timothy Harvey)

2006 *SET UP/SITUATION LIVE*
duet performance
Centre nationale de la danse, Paris, 18–19 May
Performers—Deanne Butterworth, Timothy Harvey
Sound score—François Tétaz

2006 *SET UP/SITUATION LIVE*
duet performance
Siobhan Davies Studios, London, 24–25 May
Performers—Deanne Butterworth, Timothy Harvey
Sound score—François Tétaz

2006 *The Idea of It*
solo performance
Anna Schwartz Gallery, Melbourne, 20–22 Oct
Costumes—Kara Baker and Shelley Lasica for PROJECT
Sound score—Milo Kossowski

2006 *Play in a Room*
ensemble performance
Hoopla Room, Malthouse Theatre, Melbourne, 26–27 Nov
Performers—Deanne Butterworth, Timothy Harvey, Jacob Lehrer, Jo Lloyd, Bronwyn Ritchie, Kylie Walters
Costumes—Shelley Lasica

2006 *Pieces from Another Piece*
ensemble performance
Lucy Guerin Inc Studios, Melbourne, 6–10 Dec
Presented as part of *Pieces for Small Spaces*
Performers—Deanne Butterworth, Timothy Harvey, Jo Lloyd, Bronwyn Ritchie

2007

2007 *Play in a Room*
ensemble performance
Third Floor Studio, Joyce SoHo,
New York City, 19–21 Jan
Presented as part of the APAP
(Association of Performing Arts Presenters)
annual conference program
Performers—Deanne Butterworth, Shelley Lasica, Timothy Harvey, Jo Lloyd
Costumes—Shelley Lasica

2007 *Play in a Room*
ensemble performance, 35 minutes
Dancehouse, Melbourne, 13–14 Dec
Performers—Deanne Butterworth, Timothy Harvey, Shelley Lasica, Jo Lloyd
Costumes—Compiled by Shelley Lasica; garments by Richard Nylon (originally for *History Situation*), ALPHA60 and Kara Baker and Shelley Lasica for PROJECT
Sound score—Milo Kossowski

2008

2008 *VIANNE*
ensemble performance, 50 minutes
fortyfivedownstairs, Melbourne, 3–14 Dec
Performers—Deanne Butterworth, Timothy Harvey, Jo Lloyd, Bonnie Paskas, Lee Serle
Mise-en-scène—Anne-Marie May
Costumes—Kara Baker and Shelley Lasica for PROJECT
Music—Milo Kossowski and Morgan McWaters for PEACE OUT!
Lighting and design consultant—Bluebottle (Ben Cobham)
Invitation design—Milo Kossowski
Text for program notes—Fiona Hile
Curatorium—Ben Speth, Milo Kossowski, Robyn McKenzie, Anne-Marie May
Diffusion—Rachel Young
Project management—Moriarty's Project Inc
Photography—Rohan Young
Production management—Bluebottle (Bernadette Sweeney and Adam Hardy)
Technical operation—Jenny Hector
Interns—Holly Durant, Kelly Jirsa, Madeleine Krenek, Shian Law

2009 Teaches choreography in Melbourne at Lucy Guerin Inc; School of Art, Monash Art, Design and Architecture, Monash University; Interior Design, RMIT University; Victorian College of the Arts and the Grimwade Centre for Cultural Materials Conservation, both University of Melbourne; and in Sydney at the Faculty of the Arts and Social Sciences, University of NSW

2009 *VIANNE*
ensemble performance, 50 minutes
Dancehouse, Melbourne, 10–11 Mar
Performers—Deanne Butterworth, Timothy Harvey, Jo Lloyd, Bonnie Paskas, Lee Serle
Mise-en-scène—Anne-Marie May
Costumes—Kara Baker and Shelley Lasica for PROJECT
Music—Milo Kossowski and Morgan McWaters for PEACE OUT!
Text for program notes—Fiona Hile
Curatorium—Ben Speth, Milo Kossowski, Robyn McKenzie, Anne-Marie May
Project management—Moriarty's Project Inc

2009 *FULL COLOUR*
ensemble performance
Chunky Move, Melbourne, 10–13 Dec
Performers—Deanne Butterworth, Kyle Kremerskothen, Shelley Lasica
Wildcard performers—Phillip Adams, Helen Herbertson, Jo Lloyd, Trevor Patrick
Producer—Moriarty's Project Inc
Production management—Bluebottle (Bernadette Sweeney)
Costumes—Shelley Lasica
Sound score—Milo Kossowski, Morgan McWaters
Lighting—Bluebottle (Ben Cobham)
Diffusion—Rachel Young
Graphic design—Milo Kossowski
Technical support—Rose Connors Dance

2009 Shelley Lasica and Deanne Butterworth
DUELLE
duet performance
Centre for Contemporary Photography, Melbourne, 18 Dec
Performers—Shelley Lasica, Deanne Butterworth

2010 No title
trio performance
Dancehouse, Melbourne, 7 May
Presented as part of *24 Hours*, curated by Jo Lloyd
Performers—Derrick Amanatidis, Kyle Kremerskothen, Lee Serle
Costumes and set design—Belinda Hellier
Sound score—Milo Kossowski

2010 Residency, Lieu d'Art Contemporain, Narbonne, France (with Deborah Saxon)

2010 *Something Happens*
duet performance
Lieu d'Art Contemporain, Narbonne, France, 16 Jul
Performers—Shelley Lasica, Deborah Saxon

2011 Devises Nestnet, a mentorship program for five dancers to create their own solo work while participating in the development of *COLLECT*, a new work by Shelley Lasica. Dancers: Natalie Abbott, Tim Darbyshire, Kelly Jirsa, Lily Paskas, Brooke Stamp

2011 *FULL COLOUR*
ensemble performance, 30 minutes
Critical Path, Sydney, 17 Sep
Presented as part of SEAM 2011
Performers—Deanne Butterworth, Kyle Kremerskothen, Shelley Lasica
Producer—Moriarty's Project Inc
Costumes—Shelley Lasica
Sound score—Milo Kossowski, Morgan McWaters

2012 Contributes choreography to Helen Grogan, *INSIDE THURSDAY—VIANNE AGAIN* (*Drawing Room D112, MADA*) 2012
ensemble performance and video installation
3-channel HD digital video, 2-channel sound, spatialised for site; 5 minutes 50 seconds, looped
Drawing Room D112, School of Art, Monash University Caulfield campus, Melbourne, 7 Sep
online video and photographs
10 digital photographs, HD digital video; 5 minutes 47 seconds, Vimeo online platform
Video and photographic documentation—Anna Gilby and Helen Grogan
Choreography—Shelley Lasica
Performers—Deanne Butterworth, Timothy Harvey, Jo Lloyd, Bonnie Paskas
Objects—Anne-Marie May
Wardrobe—Shelley Lasica
Sound score—Milo Kossowski, Morgan McWaters

2011 *COLLECT*
ensemble performance
Bagging Room, Malthouse Theatre, Melbourne, 26–27 Nov
Presented as part of the Nestnet mentorship program
Performers—Natalie Abbott, Deanne Butterworth, Tim Darbyshire, Kelly Jirsa, Shelley Lasica, Lily Paskas, Lee Serle, Brooke Stamp, John Utans
Producer—Moriarty's Project Inc
Production manager—Katie Sfetkidis
Set design—Belinda Hellier
Projections—Rohan Young
Costumes—Belinda Hellier
Sound score—Milo Kossowski

2012 Member, Board of Directors, Dancehouse, Melbourne

2012 *VIANNE AGAIN*
ensemble performance
Drawing Room D112, School of Art, Monash University Caulfield campus, Melbourne, 6 Sep
Performers—Deanne Butterworth, Timothy Harvey, Jo Lloyd, Bonnie Paskas
Mise-en-scène—Anne-Marie May
Wardrobe—Shelley Lasica
Sound score—Milo Kossowski, Morgan McWaters

2012 *VIANNE AGAIN*
ensemble performance
Iwaki Auditorium, ABC Southbank Centre, Melbourne, 15 Sep
Performers—Deanne Butterworth, Timothy Harvey, Jo Lloyd, Bonnie Paskas
Mise-en-scène—Anne-Marie May
Wardrobe—Shelley Lasica
Sound score—Milo Kossowski, Morgan McWaters, Antuong Nguyen

2013 With Helen Grogan, facilitates Choreography and Related Thinking (CART), a practice-focused discussion group for independent choreographers involving research and theory related to performance, choreography and dance

2013 *Hallo*
duet performance, 10 minutes
Aesop North Melbourne, 22 Mar
Presented as part of *Action/Response* by Arts House and Hannah Mathews for Dance Massive
Performers—Shelley Lasica, Daniel Newell

2013 Tony Clark and Shelley Lasica
Represent
performance with scenery
Galerie Seippel, Cologne, 3 Aug
Performer—Shelley Lasica

2013 *VIANNE AGAIN*
ensemble performance
RMIT Design Hub, Melbourne, 5 Sep
Performers—Deanne Butterworth, Timothy Harvey, Jo Lloyd, Bonnie Paskas
Mise-en-scène—Anne-Marie May
Wardrobe—Shelley Lasica
Sound score—Milo Kossowski, Morgan McWaters

2014 Performs in Bridie Lunney, *This Endless Becoming* 2013
installation and performance
National Gallery of Victoria, Melbourne, 15 Feb
Presented as part of Melbourne Now, 22 Nov 2013 – 23 Mar 2014
Performers—Sarah Enright, Melanie Lane, Shelley Lasica, James Lunney, Torie Nimmervoll, Lily Paskas

2014 Performs in Bridie Lunney, *There is a way, if we want, into everything* 2014
installation and performance
Melbourne Art Fair Project Space, Royal Exhibition Building, 13 Aug
Presented by Gertrude Contemporary
Performers—Lily Paskas, Torie Nimmervoll, Shelley Lasica

2014 Performs in Alicia Frankovich, *Defending Plural Experiences* 2014
performance
Australian Centre for Contemporary Art, Melbourne, 11 Oct
Presented as part of the exhibition *Framed Movements*, curated by Hannah Mathews
Performers—Sheryl Bryce, Kate Cooke, Dominic Edwards-Brown, Kien Fai, Annie Fayzdaughter, Gaston Freddi, Aurelia Guo, Yvette Grant, Vivienne Halat, Penny Hale, Fabion Kauker, Mick Klepner Roe, Shelley Lasica, Blane Muntz, Ellie Nikakis, Phil Novakovic, Patarawan Phumnikhom, Joanne Presser, Megan Sayce, Noon Silk, Brett Smith, Lilian Steiner, Ainslie Templeton

2014 ANAT Synapse Art/Science Residency, Centre for Eye Research, University of Melbourne, involving the research project *Sight and Perception in Dance*, Jun–Nov, with Deanne Butterworth and Jo Lloyd

2013 *AS WE MAKE IT*
solo performance
Minanoie, Melbourne, 16 Nov
Producer—Paris Paphitis
Sound score—François Tétaz
Lighting—Rose Connors Dance

2013 Shelley Lasica, Anne-Marie May and Helen Grogan
INSIDE VIANNE AGAIN (*National Gallery of Victoria*)
ensemble performance and video installation
2-channel HD digital video, 4-channel sound; single-channel HD digital video, sound; 12 minutes, looped
National Gallery of Victoria, Melbourne, 22 Nov 2013 – 23 Mar 2014
Presented as part of Melbourne Now
Performers—Deanne Butterworth, Timothy Harvey, Jo Lloyd, Bonnie Paskas
Videographer and camera technician—Anna Gilby
Camera technician—Laura May Grogan
NGV sound design—Benjamin Walbrook
Wardrobe—Shelley Lasica

2014 *AS WE MAKE IT*
solo performance
National Gallery of Victoria, Melbourne, 23 Feb
Presented in the February Solo Series as part of Melbourne Now
Producer—Paris Paphitis
Sound score—François Tétaz

2014 Tony Clark and Shelley Lasica
Represent
performance with scenery
Murray White Room, Melbourne, 6 Mar
Performer—Shelley Lasica

2014 *AS WE MAKE IT*
solo performance
Arts House, Melbourne, 14–30 Mar
Presented as part of the Festival of Live Art
Producer—Paris Paphitis
Sound score—François Tétaz
Lighting—Rose Connors Dance

2014 Tony Clark and Shelley Lasica
Represent
performance with scenery
Private residence, Militello in Val Catania, Italy, 17 Apr
Performer—Shelley Lasica

2014 *AS WE MAKE IT*
solo performance
Australian Centre for Contemporary Art, Melbourne, 19 Nov
Presented as part of the series *SPECIFIC IN-BETWEEN (the choreographic negotiated in six parts)* by Helen Grogan for the exhibition *Framed Movements*
Producer—Paris Paphitis
Sound score—François Tétaz
Lighting—Rose Connors Dance

2015 Performs in Ben Speth, *Iliads* 2015
a performance of books 1–4 of *The Iliad*
upstairs loft, 36 Moreland Street, Footscray, Melbourne, 12–14 Feb
Performers—Nana Biluš Abaffy, Natalie Abbott, Sarah Aiken, Rebecca Jensen, Shelley Lasica, Maud Léger, Kevin Lo, Bagryana Popov, Philipa Rothfield, Greg Zuccolo

2015 Performs in Bridie Lunney, *Desire Will Not Hold* 2015
installation and performance
Artspace, Sydney, 27 and 29 Mar
Presented as part of *An Imprecise Science*, 28 Mar – 24 May
Performers—Shelley Lasica, Brooke Stamp

2015 Performs in Helen Grogan, *CONCERT 2. Redistributing view (installing gaps)* 2015
sculptural installation and performance
West Space, Melbourne, 20 Jun
Presented as part of Helen Grogan's solo exhibition *Three Adjoining Spaces with Manifold Edges*
Performers—Deanne Butterworth, Helen Grogan, Simon MacEwan, Shelley Lasica

2016 Fayen d'Evie and Shelley Lasica, with Irina Povolotskaya
Tactile Dialogues [*Shared Action*] 2016
participatory performance
Presented as part of *Human Commonalities*, V.A.C. and the State Museum of Vadim Sidur, Moscow, 10 Sep – 30 Oct

2014 Tony Clark and Shelley Lasica
Represent
performance with scenery
National Arboretum, Canberra, 13 Dec
Performer—Shelley Lasica

2015 *Solos for Other People*
ensemble performance, 50 minutes
Carlton Baths Stadium, Melbourne, 13–22 Mar
Presented as part of Dance Massive 2015
Performers—Natalie Abbott, Deanne Butterworth, Timothy Harvey, Shelley Lasica, Jo Lloyd, Daniel Newell, Bonnie Paskas, Lily Paskas, Deborah Saxon, Lee Serle, Kylie Walters
Producers—Kara Ward, Kyle Kremerskothen
Stage manager—Amy Bagshaw
Composition—Anne-Marie May
Costumes—Belinda Hellier
Sound score—Milo Kossowski
Lighting—Rose Connors Dance

2015 Shelley Lasica and Katie Lee
The Possibility of Performance
duet performance
Margaret Lawrence Gallery, Melbourne, 21 Mar
Presented as part of *The Object as Score*
Performers—Shelley Lasica, Katie Lee

2015 Shelley Lasica, Deanne Butterworth and Jo Lloyd
How Choreography Works
exhibition and ensemble performance, 60 minutes
West Space, Melbourne, 9 Oct, 24 Oct, 6–7 Nov
Performers—Deanne Butterworth, Shelley Lasica (primary performer), Jo Lloyd
Producer—Kara Ward
Video selection—Deanne Butterworth, Jo Lloyd
Video editing—Duane Morrison
Object—Shelley Lasica (design), Tom Burless (fabrication)

2015 *Solos for Other People Reimagined—Summer Edition*
ensemble performance
RMIT Design Hub, Dec
Performers—Deanne Butterworth, Shelley Lasica (primary performer), Jo Lloyd, Daniel Newell, Bonnie Paskas, Lee Serle
Producers—Kara Ward, Kyle Kremerskothen
Composition—Anne-Marie May
Costumes—Belinda Hellier
Sound score—Milo Kossowski

2016 Shelley Lasica, Deanne Butterworth and Jo Lloyd
How How Choreography Works
ensemble performance, 60 minutes
Art Gallery of New South Wales, Sydney, 27 Apr
Presented as part of *Choreography and the Gallery,* 20th Biennale of Sydney and UNSW Sydney
Performers—Deanne Butterworth, Shelley Lasica, Jo Lloyd

2016 No title
solo performance
Blindside, Melbourne, 30 Jul
Presented by Liquid Architecture and Blindside for the exhibition *Gesture Manifest*

2017 Fayen d'Evie, Shelley Lasica and Bryan Phillips
Story, as told. 2017
performance
Ian Potter Museum of Art, University of Melbourne, 7 Oct
Presented as part of the exhibition *The Score*, curated by Jacqueline Doughty

2017 Performs in Bridie Lunney, *Fold* 2017
sculptural installation and performance
Performers—Deanne Butterworth, Shelley Lasica, Torie Nimmervoll, Lilian Steiner
Federation Square, Melbourne, 17, 18, 24, 25 Nov
Presented as part of the Melbourne Prize for Urban Sculpture 2017, 13–27 Nov

2016 *The Shape of Things to Come*
solo performance
The Hotel Windsor, Melbourne, 18–21 Aug
Presented as part of *Room 301* at SPRING 1883, performance series curated by Mark Feary
Performer—Shelley Lasica
Producer—Zoe Theodore
Costumes—Belinda Hellier

2017 Residency, Artspace, Sydney

2017 *The Design Plot*
durational ensemble performance
MPavilion, Melbourne, 28 Jan
Performers—Ellen Davies, Timothy Harvey, Louella May Hogan, Shelley Lasica, Daniel Newell, Lilian Steiner, Jo White
Producer—Zoe Theodore
Wardrobe—Shelley Lasica

2017 *The Shape of Things to Come*
solo performance
Artspace, Sydney, 9 Feb
Presented as part of *Superposition of Three Types*, 9 Feb – 17 Apr
Producer—Zoe Theodore
Costume—Belinda Hellier

2017 *The Design Plot*
durational ensemble performance
Gertrude Glasshouse, Melbourne, 23 Feb – 4 Mar
Performers—Ellen Davies, Timothy Harvey, Louella May Hogan, Shelley Lasica, Daniel Newell, Lilian Steiner, Jo White
Producer—Zoe Theodore
Wardrobe—Shelley Lasica

2017 *The Design Plot*
durational ensemble performance
RMIT Design Hub, Melbourne, 3 Mar
Presented as part of the exhibition *High Risk Dressing / Critical Fashion*
Performers—Ellen Davies, Timothy Harvey, Louella May Hogan, Shelley Lasica, Daniel Newell, Lilian Steiner, Jo White
Producer—Zoe Theodore
Wardrobe—Shelley Lasica

2017 *The Design Plot*
durational ensemble performance
Minanoie, Melbourne, 13 May
Performers—Ellen Davies, Timothy Harvey, Louella May Hogan, Shelley Lasica, Daniel Newell, Lilian Steiner, Jo White
Producer—Zoe Theodore
Wardrobe—Shelley Lasica

2017 *BEHAVIOUR Part 1*
video documentation from the performance at Store 5 exhibited in *Every Brilliant Eye: Australian Art of the 1990s*
The Ian Potter Centre: NGV Australia, Melbourne, 2 Jun – 1 Oct

2018 Contributes to Helen Grogan, *splitting open the surface on which it is inscribed (Shelley)* 2018
multi-channel video and sound recording, synchronised and looped, with spatialised configuration; 14 minutes 50 seconds
Developed for the exhibition *Great Movements of Feeling*, Gertrude Contemporary, Melbourne, 11 May – 16 Jun, curated by Zara Sigglekow
Choreographic score design and development—Helen Grogan
Choreographic score enaction for Gertrude Contemporary foyer site—Shelley Lasica
Sound recordist—Liam Power
Participants in 2018 'Lilac' session/discourse for Artery studio site—Atong Atem, Jess Gall, Laura May Grogan, Simon MacEwan, Liam Power

2018 Contributes to Fayen d'Evie, *FROM DUST TO DUST: PROLOGUE*
Castlemaine Gaol, Dja Dja Wurrung Country, 19 May
hybrid artist-curatorial project, inviting experimentation and conversations among Jen Bervin, Simon Charles, Gabriel Curtin, Zeno d'Evie, Benjamin Hancock, Shelley Lasica, Adam Leslie, Bryan Phillips, Pippa Samaya, Anna Seymour, Ravi Vasavan and Katie West, and, in absentia, Jennifer Justice, Aaron McPeake, Lucreccia Quintanilla and Andy Slater
Welcome to Country—Uncle Rick Nelson and Aunty Paulette Nelson
Afternoon tea—Murnong Mammas

2017 *The Design Plot*
video, 49 minutes
from the performance staged at the Royal Melbourne Tennis Club, Melbourne
Performers—Ellen Davies, Timothy Harvey, Louella May Hogan, Shelley Lasica, Daniel Newell, Lilian Steiner, Jo White
Director and editor—James Wright
Camera—James Wright, Eugene Perepletchikov
Sound recordist—Benjamin Walbrook
Wardrobe—Shelley Lasica
Producer—Zoe Theodore

2017 *The Shape of Things to Come*
solo performance
Neon Parc, Melbourne, 7 Oct
Presented as part of the exhibition *I Love Pat Larter*, 26 Aug – 14 Oct
Producer—Zoe Theodore
Costumes—Belinda Hellier

2018 Residency, The Substation, Melbourne

2018 Residency, Gertrude Glasshouse, Melbourne

2018 Ten-day research residency with Helen Grogan, during Grogan's residency with AIR—ARTIST IN RESIDENCE Niederösterreich, Krems, Austria

2018 Chair, Board of Directors, Dancehouse, Melbourne

2018 *BEHAVIOUR Part 7*
ensemble performance, 20 minutes
Union House, University of Melbourne, 3 Feb
Performers—Deanne Butterworth, Ellen Davies, LJ Connolly-Hiatt, Timothy Harvey, Alice Heyward, Louella May Hogan, Benjamin Hurley, Rebecca Jensen, Leah Landau, Shelley Lasica, Jo Lloyd, Caroline Meaden, Daniel Newell, Megan Payne, Bronwyn Ritchie, Harrison Ritchie-Jones, Lilian Steiner, Jo White
Producer—Zoe Theodore

2018 *The Design Plot*
durational ensemble performance
MPavilion, Melbourne, 4 Feb
Performers—Ellen Davies, Timothy Harvey, Louella May Hogan, Shelley Lasica, Daniel Newell, Lilian Steiner, Jo White
Producer—Zoe Theodore
Costumes—Shelley Lasica

2018 *Dimensional*
solo performance
Chapter House Lane, Melbourne, 22 Mar
Presented as part of 'Tall Buildings: Their Problems and Some Ideas', symposium program presented by Molonglo in collaboration with the National Gallery of Victoria for Melbourne Design Week 2018
Producer—Zoe Theodore
Costume—Belinda Hellier

2018 *The Design Plot*
durational ensemble performance
Sutton Projects, Melbourne, 26–28 Apr
Performers—Ellen Davies, Timothy Harvey, Louella May Hogan, Shelley Lasica, Daniel Newell, Lilian Steiner, Jo White
Projections—James Wright
Producer—Zoe Theodore
Wardrobe—Shelley Lasica

2018 *The Design Plot*
durational ensemble performance
The Substation, Melbourne, 11–14 Jul
Performers—Ellen Davies, Timothy Harvey, Louella May Hogan, Shelley Lasica, Daniel Newell, Lilian Steiner, Jo White
Projections—James Wright
Producer—Zoe Theodore
Wardrobe—Shelley Lasica

2018 *The Design Plot*
durational ensemble performance
215 Albion Street, Brunswick, Melbourne, 12 Jul
Performers—Ellen Davies, Timothy Harvey, Louella May Hogan, Shelley Lasica, Daniel Newell, Lilian Steiner, Jo White
Producer—Zoe Theodore
Wardrobe—Shelley Lasica

2018 *Greater Union*
durational duet performance
The Substation, Melbourne, 29 Jul
Performers—Timothy Harvey, Shelley Lasica
Video projection—Callum Morton (originally produced for *RESTRICTED SITUATION* 1999)
Objects—Anne-Marie May (originally produced for *VIANNE* 2008)
Producer—Zoe Theodore
Wardrobe—Shelley Lasica

2018 Tony Clark and Shelley Lasica
Represent
performance with scenery
11m2, Berlin, 3 Aug
Performer—Shelley Lasica

2018 *BEHAVIOUR Part 7*
ensemble performance, 30 minutes
215 Albion Street, Brunswick, Melbourne, 8 Sep
Presented as part of *TO DO / TO MAKE*, curated by Shelley Lasica and Zoe Theodore in association with Neon Parc
Performers—Deanne Butterworth, Ellen Davies, LJ Connolly-Hiatt, Luke Fryer, Timothy Harvey, Alice Heyward, Louella May Hogan, Benjamin Hurley, Rebecca Jensen, Leah Landau, Shelley Lasica, Jo Lloyd, Caroline Meaden, Daniel Newell, Megan Payne, Bronwyn Ritchie, Harrison Ritchie-Jones, Lilian Steiner, Jo White
Producer—Zoe Theodore

2018 *Greater Union*
durational duet performance, 60 minutes
215 Albion Street, Brunswick, Melbourne, 21 Oct
Presented as part of *TO DO / TO MAKE 2*, curated by Shelley Lasica and Zoe Theodore in association with Neon Parc
Performers—Timothy Harvey, Shelley Lasica
Video projection—Callum Morton (originally produced for *RESTRICTED SITUATION* 1999)
Objects—Anne-Marie May (originally produced for *VIANNE* 2008)
Producer—Zoe Theodore
Wardrobe—Shelley Lasica

2019 Performs in Jo Lloyd, *LIVE JUNK*
performance
Idea Studios, Melbourne, 26 Feb
Performers—Sarah Aiken, Deanne Butterworth, Anika de Ruyter, Sophie Gargan, Sheridan Gerrard, Hillary Goldsmith, Rebecca Jensen, Melanie Lane, Shelley Lasica, Shian Law, Claire Leske, Jo Lloyd, Will McBride, Amber McCartney, Emma Riches, Harrison Ritchie-Jones, Rachael Wisby, Thomas Woodman
Costumes and styling—Andrew Treloar
Music composition—Duane Morrison
Producer—Michaela Coventry (Sage Arts)

2019 Performs in David Rosetzky, *Composite Acts*
one-night exhibition, performance and video
Abbotsford Convent, Melbourne, 21 Sep
Commissioned by Channels Festival
Performers—Shelley Lasica, Harrison Ritchie-Jones (live performance); Arabella Frahn-Starkie, Shelley Lasica, Harrison Ritchie-Jones (video)
Choreography (performance and video)—Jo Lloyd
Sculptural set/set design—Sean Meilak (performance and video)
Sound designer/composer—Duane Morrison (performance and video)
Cinematographer—Katie Milwright
Video editor—James Wright
Video producer—Eyvonne Carfora
Sound recordist—Steven Bond
1st Camera assistant and focus puller—Redmond Stevenson
2nd Camera assistant—Shang-Lien Yang
Wardrobe assistant—Daniel Hindson
Additional costume—Nita-Jane McMahon
Additional props—Anne Kucera
Colour by—Crayon
Colourist—Daniel Stonehouse
Compositing—Lumberfly
Compositor—Josh Thomas
Filmed at—Idea Studios, Brunswick

2019

2019 Residency and exhibition for Concurrent Castings—Pferd Research, a research project undertaken by Helen Grogan and Shelley Lasica at PFERD Forum for Contemporary Art, Vienna, 27 May – 15 Jun

2019 Residency, Bus Projects, Melbourne

2019 *If I Don't Understand You*
ensemble performance, 40 minutes
Temperance Hall, Melbourne, 26–28 Sep
Presented as part of Melbourne Fringe
Performers—LJ Connolly-Hiatt, Luke Fryer, Shelley Lasica, Megan Payne, Lana Šprajcer
Producer—Zoe Theodore
Mise-en-scène—Colby Vexler
Stage manager/production—Meri Leeworthy
Sound score—Milo Kossowski

2019 Shelley Lasica with Martin Grant
DRESS (first performed 1998)
solo performance
Anna Schwartz Gallery, Melbourne, 8–9 Nov
Presented as part of the exhibition *Never the Same River* for the Melbourne International Arts Festival

2019 *The Design Plot*
durational ensemble performance
Bus Projects, Melbourne, 30 Nov
Performers: Ellen Davies, Timothy Harvey, Louella May Hogan, Shelley Lasica, Daniel Newell, Lilian Steiner, Jo White
Producer—Zoe Theodore
Wardrobe—Shelley Lasica

2019 *The Thing I Want*
video, 5 minutes
Immigration Museum, Melbourne, 2 Dec 2019 – 29 Feb 2020
Presented as part of *Dance Reel*, curated by Amrita Hepi and Zoe Theodore
Choreography—Shelley Lasica
Performers—LJ Connolly-Hiatt, Shelley Lasica, Megan Payne
Director—Antuong Nguyen
Producer—Zoe Theodore
Cinematography—Joey Knox
Composer—Milo Kossowski
Mise-en-scène—Colby Vexler

2019 *If I Don't Understand You*
ensemble performance, 40 minutes
Neon Parc, Melbourne, 5 Dec
Performers—LJ Connolly-Hiatt, Luke Fryer, Shelley Lasica, Megan Payne, Lana Šprajcer
Producer—Zoe Theodore
Mise-en-scène—Colby Vexler
Sound score—Milo Kossowski
Wardrobe—Shelley Lasica

2020 *The Design Plot*
ensemble performance
Immigration Museum, Melbourne, 9 Feb
Curated by Amrita Hepi and Zoe Theodore for the *Summer of Dance* series, 2019–20
Performers—Ellen Davies, Timothy Harvey, Shelley Lasica, Daniel Newell, Lilian Steiner, Jo White
Producer—Zoe Theodore
Wardrobe—Shelley Lasica

2021 Performs in David Rosetzky, *Composite Acts* exhibition and lived-streamed performance, involving the video and sculptural set-pieces that were part of the initial 2019 event, and a series of photographs featuring Lasica
Presented as part of the festival PHOTO 2021
Sutton Gallery, Melbourne, 6 Feb – 6 Mar; performances 6 Mar
Performers—Arabella Frahn-Starkie, Shelley Lasica, Harrison Ritchie-Jones
Choreography—Jo Lloyd

2020 *Greater Union*
durational duet performance, 120 minutes
257 Albert Street, Brunswick, Melbourne, 15 Feb
Presented in association with Nine Buildings
Performers—Timothy Harvey, Shelley Lasica
Video projection—Callum Morton
(originally produced for *RESTRICTED SITUATION* 1999) Objects—Anne-Marie May
(originally produced for *VIANNE* 2008)
Producer—Zoe Theodore
Wardrobe—Shelley Lasica

2020 Shelley Lasica and Meri Blavezski
If I Don't Understand You
video, 15 minutes
Screened at Federation Square, Melbourne, 7–13 Dec
Performers—LJ Connolly-Hiatt, Luke Fryer, Shelley Lasica, Megan Payne, Lana Šprajcer
Producer—Zoe Theodore
Mise-en-scène—Colby Vexler
Sound score—Milo Kossowski
Wardrobe—Shelley Lasica

2021 Recipient of an Australia Council Fellowship for Dance

2021 Primary research associate, *Precarious Movements: Choreography and the Museum*, a three-year research project with partners University of New South Wales, National Gallery of Victoria, Tate UK, Art Gallery of New South Wales and Monash University Museum of Art, supported by an Australian Research Council Linkage Grant

2021 Shelley Lasica and Deanne Butterworth
DUELLE (first performed 2009)
duet performance
The Pavilion, Fitzroy Gardens, Melbourne, 20 Mar
Presented as part of Deanne Butterworth's artist residency at The Pavilion
Performers—Shelley Lasica, Deanne Butterworth

2022 2022

2022 *Hide Technique*
single-channel video; 6 minutes 14 seconds
Caves, Melbourne, 4–26 Feb
Presented as part of the exhibition *Communal Atmosphere or The Space The Air (Falls) behind you as you move,* curated by Rozalind Drummond

2022 *WHEN I AM NOT THERE*
performance-exhibition
Monash University Museum of Art, Melbourne, 16–27 Aug, curated by Hannah Mathews
Including *WHEN I AM NOT THERE* 2022
ensemble performance with sound, costumes, nautical net, movable screen and a selection of existing contributions from others
Performers—LJ Connolly-Hiatt, Luke Fryer, Timothy Harvey, Rebecca Jensen, Shelley Lasica, Megan Payne, Oliver Savariego, Lana Šprajcer
Creative producer—Zoe Theodore
Consultants—Lisa Radford, Colby Vexler
Sound score—François Tétaz (composition) from scores by François Tétaz and Milo Kossowski commissioned for earlier works by Shelley Lasica
Works by—Tony Clark (scenery originally produced for *BELIEVE* 1990); Anne-Marie May (sculptures originally produced for *VIANNE* 2008 and *Solos for Other People* 2015); Callum Morton (video originally produced for *RESTRICTED SITUATION* 1999); Jacqui Shelton (video based on text originally produced for *The Design Plot* 2020); Kathy Temin (costume originally produced for *CHARACTER X* 1996); Roger Wood (maquette originally produced for *History Situation* 2002)
Costumes—Kara Baker and Shelley Lasica for PROJECT, Martin Grant, Belinda Hellier, Margaret Lasica, Margaret and Shelley Lasica, Shelley Lasica, Richard Nylon, Shio Otani, Fiona Scanlan
References to previous works by Shelley Lasica and ongoing research—Shelley Lasica (video research material, vinyl flooring), Robyn McKenzie (script), Kerstin Thompson Architects (circulation map)*, Roger Wood (light intervention)

2023 *WHEN I AM NOT THERE*
performance-exhibition
Art Gallery of New South Wales, Sydney, May, curated by Lisa Catt
Including *WHEN I AM NOT THERE* 2022
ensemble performance with sound, costumes, nautical net, movable screen and a selection of existing contributions from others
Contributors and components as above, except for the reference marked with *

2024

BIBLIOGRAPHY

Anderson, Jack, 'Carrying On, Rain Checks Not Necessary', *The New York Times*, 12 July 1997, p. 16.

Avdi, Faruk, 'Aloof Inner Being', *Theatre Australasia*, no. 7, July 1994, p. 15.

Boyd, Chris, 'Believe: Solo Dance by Shelley Lasica', *The Melbourne Times*, 5 December 1990, p. 17.

Boztas, Senay, 'The Secret Language of Dance', *The Age*, 1 December 2008, p. 14.

Brannigan, Erin, 'Positively Unassertive: Dancing in the Art Gallery of NSW', *Broadsheet Journal*, no. 45.2, 2016, pp. 26–29.

———, 'Context, Discipline, and Understanding: The Poetics of Shelley Lasica's Gallery-Based Work', in Erin Brannigan, Hannah Mathews and Caroline Wake (eds), *Performance Paradigm*, 'Performance, Choreography, and the Gallery', vol. 13, 2017, pp. 97–117.

Breen Burns, Janice, 'Movers and Shakers', *The Age*, 20 March 2002, p. 4.

Carroll, Steven, 'Stage Whisper', *The Age*, 24 May 1996, Entertainment Guide, p. 11.

Christofis, Lee, 'Help, Grind, Downloading, Character X', *The Australian*, 31 May 1996, p. 17.

———, 'Exit in a Minor Key', *The Australian*, 17 July 1998, p. 15.

Clemens, Justin, 'VIANNE, VIANNE, again; or, the some another', exh. cat., Dancehouse, Melbourne, 2008.

Crampton, Hilary, 'A Dressing Down in the Name of Art', *The Age*, 16 February 1998, p. 5.

———, 'Chance Discoveries in Dance', *The Age*, 15 December 2007.

Dunphy, Kim, 'When Actions Speak Louder than Words', *The Age*, 17 February 1999.

Elliott, Helen, 'Taking Cringe Out of Artistic Dance', *The Age*, 23 January 1995.

Ellis, Justine and Dan Rule (eds), *The Design Plot*, Perimeter Editions, Melbourne, 2021.

Fairfax, Vicki, 'Dance Does Not Yield Its Secrets', *The Age*, 28 May 1996.

Farmer, Alison, 'Noiseless Movement', *The Bulletin*, 3 August 1993, pp. 83–84.

Feary, Mark, 'Waiting for Duelle', *Shelley Lasica and Deanne Butterworth: Duelle*, Centre for Contemporary Photography, Melbourne, 2008, https://ccp.org.au/exhibitions/all/duelle-2009.

Fensham, Rachel, 'Studio Practices 1: Extensions: Room to Move', interview with Shelley and Wendy Lasica, *RealTime*, no. 9, October–November 1995, p. 36.

Fisher, Lynn, 'Cool Lasica Hints at Complexities', *The West Australian*, 24 July 1993, p. 52.

Fraser, Susie, 'Sight and Vision', *Writings on Dance*, no. 2, Spring 1987, p. 49.

Fuhrmann, Andrew, 'Dance Massive Review Wrap (Solos for Other People and The Boom Project)', *Daily Review*, 16 March 2005, https://dailyreview.com.au/dance-massive-review-wrap-solos-for-other-people-and-the-boom-project/.

Gill, Harbant, 'Lasica's Joy—There's No Room at the Room in New York', *Herald Sun*, 29 January 2007, p. 81.

Glickman, Stephanie, 'Throw Caution to the Wind', *Herald Sun*, 16 February 1999.

———, 'History's Power and Tension', *Herald Sun*, 20 March 2002, p. 60.

Harley, James, 'Shelley Lasica', *Art & Text*, no. 36, May 1990, p. 147.

Hawker, Philippa, 'Curiosity Makes the Dance Fit the Audience in the Room', *The Age*, 23 November 2011, p. 17.

———, 'Shelley Lasica, Dancer and Choreographer: 11 Solos, One Work', *The Sydney Morning Herald*, 12 March 2015, https://www.smh.com.au/entertainment/dance/shelley-lasica-dancer-and-choreographer-11-solos-one-work-20150312-1421iw.html.

———, 'Dance: Together Alone. Solo Woman Works Well with Others', *The Age*, 13 March 2015, p. 30.

Hile, Fiona, untitled text, *VIANNE*, exh. cat., fortyfivedownstairs, Melbourne, 2008.

———, 'Channelling the Gaze: The Choreographic Works of Shelley Lasica', *Art & Australia*, vol. 47, no. 2, Summer 2009, pp. 242–43.

Hudson, Sarah, 'Dance of the Emotions', *Herald Sun*, 19 December 1991, p. 41.

———, 'Creative Dancing for Two', *Herald Sun*, 21 September 1999, p. 52.

Johnson, Anna, 'Dance of Life', *Vogue*, vol. 43, no. 4, April 1998.

Kelly, Eamonn, 'Detached Encounters', *The Australian*, 5 December 2008, p. 10.

Lasica, Shelley, 'Writing the Past Dance Ideologies', *Writings on Dance*, no. 2, Spring 1987, pp. 23–26.

———, *Physical Culture: A Series of Performances and an Exhibition of Visual Art*, exh. cat., 200 Gertrude Street, Fitzroy, Vic., 1989.

———, 'Retrospective', *Brolga: An Australian Journal about Dance*, no. 33, 1 December 2010, pp. 22–25.

———, 'Do You Do This Often?', in Erin Brannigan, Hannah Mathews and Caroline Wake (eds), *Performance Paradigm*, 'Performance, Choreography, and the Gallery', vol. 13, 2017, pp. 205–12.

———, 'Morning Warm Up with Shelley Lasica', in Hannah Mathews (ed.), *To Note: Notation Across Disciplines*, Perimeter Editions, Melbourne, 2017, p. 167.

Loucas, Anthea, 'Not a Dress Rehearsal', *The Age*, 8 September 1999, p. 22.
Mangan, John, 'Oddity in a Purple Fur', *The Age*, 23 May 1996.
Marshall, Jonathan, 'Action Situation', *Inpress*, no. 547, 24 February 1999.
———, 'Chunky Chops: Chunky Move's Live Acts #1', festival guide, *Melbourne Fringe*, 26 September – 17 October 1999.
Perkin, Corrie, 'Troupers Storm the Stage in the Big Apple', *The Australian*, 29 January 2007, p. 7.
Place, Belle, 'Making Modern Dance', *The Blackmail Offline*, no. 2, 2013, pp. 26–33.
Porter, Liz, 'An Unexpected Twist to Dance', *The Sunday Age*, 26 November 1989, p. 11.
Radford, Lisa, 'Whirls Colliding', *The Saturday Paper*, no. 288, 15–21 February 2020, pp. 20–21.
Renton, Andrew, 'Gaby Agis and Shelley Lasica', *Performance Magazine*, no. 65/66, Spring 1992, pp. 80–81.
Richards, Naomi, 'A Body Will Always Be a Body: Naomi Richards in Dialogue with Five Dancers in Melbourne', *RealTime*, no. 5, February–March 1995, p. 8.
Roberts, Jo, 'Revisited and Remixed: A Dance Work in Progress', *The Age*, 14 October 2005, p. 16.
Rothfield, Philipa, 'Dress, Shelley Lasica', *RealTime*, no. 24, April–May 1998, p. 40.
———, 'A Differential Tale', *RealTime*, no. 30, April–May 1999, p. 32.
———, 'Dancing Metaphysics', *RealTime*, no. 49, June–July 2002, p. 38.
———, 'Chance, Dance, Animals and the Unconscious', *RealTime*, no. 70, December 2005 – January 2006, p. 6.
———, 'Worlds Within', *RealTime*, no. 89, February–March 2009, p. 33.
———, 'No Surfaces, Only Depths', *RealTime*, no. 95, February–March 2010, p. 34.
Rule, Dan, 'Channels of Expression', *The Age*, 24 January 2015, p. 20.
———, 'Shelley Lasica / New Avenues', *VAULT*, no. 11, September 2015, pp. 36–38.
Rusher, Robin, 'Dancer's Act a Portrayal of Contemplation', *The West Australian*, 22 July 1993.
Shelley Lasica: Behaviour, exh. cat., Printed Books, Melbourne, 1994.
Shevtsova, Maria, 'Dance', *New Theatre Australia*, no. 12, September–October 1989.
Smethurst, Chloe, 'A Behind-the-Scenes Look at a Continuing Experiment', *The Age*, 18 October 2005, p. 15.
———, 'Beauty Found in Ambiguity', *The Age*, 6 December 2008, p. 21.
———, 'Dance: Collect', *The Age*, 29 November 2011, p. 15.
Smethurst, Chloe, 'Dance Review: Shelley Lasica's Solos for Other People Fills a Big Space', *The Sydney Morning Herald*, 15 March 2015, https://www.smh.com.au/entertainment/dance/dance-review-shelley-lasicas-solos-for-other-people-fills-a-big-space-20150315-144dpt.html.
Snaith, Tai, host, 'Control / Escape—A Conversation with Dancer and Choreographer Shelley Lasica', A World of One's Own (podcast), Australian Centre for Contemporary Art, Melbourne, 14 December 2017, https://soundcloud.com/acca_melbourne/a-world-of-her-own-shelley-lasica.
Soboslay, Zsuzsanna, 'Praise the Lord', *RealTime*, no. 23, February–March 1998, p. 35.
Spunner, Suzanne, 'The Thrall of the Dress: Blame it on Dior', *Art Monthly Australia*, no. 118, April 1999, pp. 14–17.
Stappmanns, Viviane, 'Shelley Lasica', *Artichoke*, no. 26, p. 76.
Studio, 'Shelley Lasica', video interview produced by Tamsen Hopkinson, *STUDIO*, un Projects, 29 March 2018, https://unprojects.org.au/article/shelley-lasica/.
Trioli, Virginia, 'Dancer Challenges Expectations of Her Audience and Invites Their Participation', *The Age*, 30 November 1990.
———, 'Dancing Here and Now', *The Age*, 11 May 1995, p. 20.
Unreich, Rachelle, 'Dancing to a New Tune', *Herald Sun*, 3 May 2003, p. 116.
Usher, Robin, 'Choreographers Tap into New York', *The Age*, 30 January 2007.
Van Schaik, Leon, 'Behaviour Patterns', *Art and Australia*, vol. 31, no. 4, Winter 1994, p. 572.

CREATIVE TEAM

LJ CONNOLLY-HIATT is a settler working as a dance maker and performer on unceded Woiwurrung Country, Naarm/Melbourne. They are a dance graduate of Unitec (Bachelor of Performing and Screen Arts), Auckland, Aotearoa New Zealand, 2015. Connolly-Hiatt makes solo and collaborative work while performing with various dance artists and companies. These include Shelley Lasica, Lilian Steiner, Chunky Move, Melanie Lane, Ellen Davies and Alice Heyward, Rebecca Jensen, and Footnote New Zealand Dance.

LUKE FRYER is an independent dance artist and arts worker based in Naarm/Melbourne. As a dance graduate of the Victorian College of the Arts he has predominantly worked with artists, including Shelley Lasica, Phoebe Robinson, Alice Will Caroline and Emma Riches, for festival and research-based projects. While completing a master's degree in arts and cultural management, Fryer is currently working between movement practice, performance and various arts organisations. His interests lie at the intersection of artistic practice, production and communication in the performing arts.

TIMOTHY HARVEY is a movement and myotherapy practitioner based in Naarm/Melbourne. His practice at the integrative health studio Truth+Body Myotherapy extends to pilates and clinical exercise. In addition to regular dance practice he connects with movement through anatomy studies, trail running and hiking. Harvey's dancing roles in the works of Shelley Lasica have spanned more than twenty years and numerous projects, including *Play in a Room*, *SET UP/ SITUATION LIVE*, *VIANNE*, *The Design Plot* and *Greater Union*.

REBECCA JENSEN is a dancer, choreographer and teacher from Aotearoa New Zealand, based in Naarm/Melbourne. Her practice considers the speculative and practical forces of dance practice, with sustained interests in multiplicity, memory, time and the influence of digital technologies. Several of her ongoing projects examine social and ecological systems through improvised group dances. In 2013, Jensen co-founded participatory project Deep Soulful Sweats with Sarah Aiken. Jensen regularly performs as a dancer; she has worked with choreographer Jo Lloyd since 2010.

MEGAN PAYNE has a bachelor's degree in dance from the Victorian College of the Arts (2013). They enjoy choreographing work with others, dancing, creating and hosting radio shows, and writing poems and stories. Payne is an associate editor with *The Suburban Review*, studies Professional Writing and Editing at RMIT University, and is writing a fiction manuscript.

LISA RADFORD explores the shared socio-political space between images, place and people. She works with others, most recently Sam George (2010–22), Yhonnie Scarce (2018–) and Shelley Lasica (2021–). Emerging from the discipline of painting, her practice traverses writing, performance, sculpture and installation. She lectures in art at the Victorian College of the Arts, University of Melbourne.

OLIVER SAVARIEGO is a contemporary dancer and choreographer based in Naarm/Melbourne. His artistic practice attempts to reconstitute and reconcile personal histories, queer identity, dance lineages, pop culture and performance modes. He has collaborated, worked and performed extensively with dancers and choreographers including Phillip Adams, Rafael Bonachela, Melanie Lane, Deanne Butterworth, Stuart Shugg and Chloe Arnott.

LANA ŠPRAJCER is a dancer and choreographer from Zagreb, Croatia, where she graduated with bachelor's degrees in contemporary dance (2016) and comparative literature (2014). She has collaborated with many artists and groups, as well as co-authored several dance and performance projects. Šprajcer enjoys questioning the nature and potential of dance to express alternative perspectives on reality.

FRANÇOIS TÉTAZ is a film composer and music producer who won the AACTA Best Original Score Award for *Judy and Punch* in 2019. He has won two Grammys, including Record of the Year at the 55th annual Grammy Awards in 2013 for his work with Gotye, and an APRA / Australian Guild of Screen Composers Award for his score for *Wolf Creek* in 2006. A regular contributor to the work of Shelley Lasica, he lives and works between Melbourne and Los Angeles, United States.

ZOE THEODORE is a Sydney-based curator, producer and writer, who has worked with Shelley Lasica since 2016. She is currently a doctoral candidate at the University of New South Wales and project coordinator for *Precarious Movements: Choreography and the Museum*. She was the co-editor of the third issue of *Dissect Journal* and has held professional roles at Anna Schwartz Gallery and the Australian Centre for Contemporary Art, Melbourne; and MoMA PS1, New York.

COLBY VEXLER is an architectural researcher and practitioner with a longstanding interest in cross-disciplinary practice. With Pricilla Heung, he leads the architecture practice Office Heuler, which began in late 2020 to extend the lines of inquiry established by the Melbourne School of Design research unit and design studio Housing, Home and Content(s): A Soft Focus on Domestic Things. He is founder and editor of the online contemporary architectural journal *cc:*.

CONTRIBUTORS

ERIN BRANNIGAN is associate professor in theatre and performance at the University of New South Wales. She is of Irish and Danish—convict, settler and political exile—descent. Her current research project, *Precarious Movements: Choreography and the Museum*, includes the associated monographs *Choreography, Visual Art and Experimental Composition 1950s–1970s* (Routledge, 2022) and *The Persistence of Dance: Choreography as Concept and Material in Contemporary Art* (Michigan University Press, forthcoming).

LISA CATT is Curator, Contemporary International Art at the Art Gallery of New South Wales, where she is working on several major commissions, performances and exhibitions for the opening of the Art Gallery's new building, Sydney Modern. Previous curatorial projects include *Get Arted: Pat Larter* (2020), co-curated with archivist Claire Eggleston; *Here We Are* (2019) and *Yona Lee: In Transit* (2018). She is currently a partner investigator on the Australian Research Council Linkage Project *Precarious Movements: Choreography in the Museum*.

JUSTIN CLEMENS writes extensively about Australian art and culture. His books include *Limericks, Philosophical and Literary* (Surpllus, 2019) and *Psychoanalysis is an Antiphilosophy* (Edinburgh, 2013). His monograph on the early colonial Australian judge Barron Field, written with T.H. Ford, will be out soon with Melbourne University Press. He is an associate professor at the University of Melbourne.

CLAUDIA LA ROCCO has written the pamphlet *Quartet* (Ugly Duckling Presse, 2020), the selected writings *The Best Most Useless Dress* (Badlands Unlimited, 2014) and *petit cadeau*, a novel published in live, digital and print editions (Chocolate Factory Theater, 2015). With musician/composer Phillip Greenlief she is animals & giraffes, an ongoing experiment in multidisciplinary improvisation. She has been a columnist for *Artforum*, a cultural critic for WNYC New York Public Radio, and in 2005–15 was a critic and reporter for the *New York Times*.

HANNAH MATHEWS is Senior Curator at MUMA, where her recent curatorial projects include *Vivienne Binns: On and through the Surface* (2022), co-curated with Anneke Jaspers; *D Harding: Through a lens of visitation* (2021); *Agatha Gothe-Snape: The Outcome Is Certain* (2020); and *Shapes of Knowledge* (2019). From 2014–16 she initiated a series of projects that engaged with choreography and the visual arts under the title Sharing Space. She is currently a chief investigator on the Australian Research Council Linkage Project *Precarious Movements: Choreography in the Museum*.

ROBYN MCKENZIE originally trained in art history. She has an established reputation as a writer on contemporary Australian art. After undertaking further study in anthropology (in the Interdisciplinary Cross-Cultural Research program at the Australian National University), her interests have focused on ways of engaging with and reactivating historical museum collections, specifically of First Nations material culture in Australian and Pacific collections. She continues to engage with and write on contemporary art.

ZOE THEODORE (see CREATIVE TEAM)

SHELLEY LASICA'S ACKNOWLEDGEMENTS

On the occasion of *WHEN I AM NOT THERE,* I would like to extend my sincere thanks to the creative team: LJ Connolly-Hiatt, Luke Fryer, Timothy Harvey, Rebecca Jensen, Megan Payne, Lisa Radford, Oliver Savariego, Lana Šprajcer, François Tétaz, Zoe Theodore and Colby Vexler; to the MUMA team, Hannah Mathews, Melissa Ratliff and Charlotte Day; to the writers and designers Erin Brannigan, Lisa Catt, Justin Clemens, Claudia La Rocco, Hannah Mathews, Robyn McKenzie, Zoe Theodore, Žiga Testen and Stuart Geddes; to Alice Mawhinney and Phoebe Kelly for their work on the archive; and to the artists who have generously lent their work for this exhibition/performance. I would also like to thank the *Precarious Movements* team for their continuing support.

I also acknowledge the support of the Australia Council Dance Fellowship I received in 2021, which has been critical in the two-year development of this project.

Thanks also, for their contributions to my work over so many years, to all the dancers, artists, designers, technicians, composers, photographers, videographers, writers and audiences, so many of whom I have engaged with and who have contributed so much to bringing performances into being; and to my ever-supportive and loving family always.

MUMA ACKNOWLEDGEMENTS

MUMA would like to thank Shelley Lasica for her trust and collaboration over the past two years as we prepared *WHEN I AM NOT THERE.*

Special thanks to creative producer Zoe Theodore and to performers and contributors LJ Connolly-Hiatt, Luke Fryer, Timothy Harvey, Rebecca Jensen, Megan Payne, Lisa Radford, Oliver Savariego, Lana Šprajcer, François Tétaz and Colby Vexler for their investment and commitment. Thanks also to Simone Tops for the design and fabrication of the movable screen.

MUMA also acknowledges the artists, writers, musicians and designers whose contributions to Shelley's past works are in conversation with the new commission: Tony Clark, Milo Kossowski, Anne-Marie May, Robyn McKenzie, Callum Morton,

Jacqui Shelton, Kathy Temin, François Tétaz and Roger Wood; and costume designers Kara Baker and Shelley Lasica for PROJECT, Martin Grant, Belinda Hellier, Margaret Lasica, Richard Nylon, Shio Otani and Fiona Scanlan.

Thanks to MUMA's staff for supporting the presentation of *WHEN I AM NOT THERE* and extending care to Shelley's team while they were with us in the galleries. The development of this project was greatly supported by Meredith Turnbull in her role as Gallery Manager in 2021 and by Monash Art, Design and Architecture for the provision of rehearsal space.

Thanks to all the writers, photographers, editors and designers for their contributions to this publication; to Curator Research Melissa Ratliff for her oversight of this monograph; to MUMA/BAHC curatorial trainee Alice Mawhinney for her research support; and to Monash University Publishing as our publishing partner.

MUMA would also like to thank our colleagues at the Art Gallery of New South Wales, in particular Lisa Catt, Maud Page, Wayne Tunnicliffe and Paschal Daantos Berry, for joining us as co-commissioners of this important project.

Lastly we extend thanks to our colleagues at the University of New South Wales (UNSW), Art Gallery of New South Wales (AGNSW), National Gallery of Victoria (NGV) and Tate UK for their support and collaboration on the project *Precarious Movements: Choreography and the Museum*, and to the Australian Research Council for the opportunity to engage in so many firsts for choreographic practice in this country: the first survey of an Australian choreographer by a museum and the first monograph of a contemporary Australian choreographer.

Precarious Movements: Choreography and the Museum is a research project involving the abovementioned partner organisations alongside MUMA. Team members include theorist Dr Erin Brannigan (UNSW); curators Lisa Catt (AGNSW), Hannah Mathews (MUMA) and Pip Wallis (NGV); conservators Louise Lawson (Tate UK) and Carolyn Murphy (AGNSW); artists Shelley Lasica and Dr Rochelle Haley (UNSW); Zoe Theodore (independent researcher) and a network of local artists, curators, archivists, museum educators, theorists and writers. This research was partially funded by the Australian Government through the Australian Research Council.

First published on the occasion of the exhibition
Shelley Lasica: WHEN I AM NOT THERE
Monash University Museum of Art, Melbourne
16–27 August 2022
Art Gallery of New South Wales, Sydney
May 2023

A catalogue record for this book is available from the National Library of Australia
Title—Shelley Lasica: WHEN I AM NOT THERE
Authors/Contributors—Erin Brannigan, Lisa Catt, Justin Clemens, Claudia La Rocco, Shelley Lasica, Hannah Mathews, Robyn McKenzie, Zoe Theodore
ISBN—9781922633347
First edition of 500 copies

Curator/editor—Hannah Mathews
Coordinating editor—Melissa Ratliff
Design—Stuart Geddes and Žiga Testen
Printing—Musumeci
Copyediting—Linda Michael
Proofreading—Clare Williamson

Cover images—Shelley Lasica, *BEHAVIOUR Part 1 and 2* 1994, Athenaeum Theatre, Melbourne, 5–7 May 1994. Photos: Roger Wood (front and back); Shelley Lasica, *The Shape of Things to Come* 2016–17, The Hotel Windsor, Melbourne, 18–21 August 2016. Photo: Mark Feary (inside cover)

Published by

MONASH University | MUMA

MONASH UNIVERSITY PUBLISHING

Monash University Museum of Art
900 Dandenong Road, Caulfield Campus
Caulfield East VIC 3145, Australia
monash.edu/muma

Monash University Publishing
Level 2, Matheson Library Annexe
44 Exhibition Walk, Clayton Campus
Wellington Road Clayton VIC 3168, Australia
publishing.monash.edu

Commission supported by

Atelier | Art Gallery NSW

Australian Government | Australia Council for the Arts

This project has been assisted by the Australian Government through the Australia Council, its arts funding and advisory body.

Australian Government
Australian Research Council

This research was partially funded by the Australian Government through the Australian Research Council (project number LP200100009).